BREAKING UP IS HARD TO DO

SUPPORT FOR PARTNERS ENDING A COMMITTED RELATIONSHIP

Ester R.A. Leutenberg & Barbara G. Feinberg, LISW-S, IMFT

100 Reproducible Activity Handouts and Educational Materials for Facilitators of Groups and Individuals

wholeperson
Stress & Wellness Publishers
Duluth, Minnesota

© 2013 WHOLE PERSON ASSOCIATES, 210 WEST MICHIGAN ST., DULUTH MN 55802-1908 • 800-247-6789

Whole Person
210 West Michigan Street
Duluth, MN 55802-1908

800-247-6789

books@wholeperson.com
www.wholeperson.com

Breaking Up Is Hard to Do
Support for partners ending a committed relationship

Copyright ©2013 by Ester A. Leutenberg and Barbara G. Feinberg. All rights reserved. Except for short excerpts for review purposes and materials in the assessment, journaling activities, and educational handouts sections, no part of this book may be reproduced or transmitted in any form by any means, electronic or mechanical without permission in writing from the publisher. Self-assessments, exercises, and educational handouts are meant to be photocopied.

All efforts have been made to ensure accuracy of the information contained in this book as of the date published. The author(s) and the publisher expressly disclaim responsibility for any adverse effects arising from the use or application of the information contained herein.

Printed in the United States of America

10 9 8 7 6 5 4 3 2 1

Editorial Director: Carlene Sippola
Art Director: Joy Morgan Dey

Library of Congress Control Number: 2013939889
ISBN: 978-1-57025-303-4

Dedication

I dedicate this book to my many clients who have shared their stories, fears and struggles with courage, candor and great generosity. I have learned so much from them and have been honored to share their journeys and, ultimately, their victories.

I have also been fortunate to work closely with other professional advisors whose wisdom, compassion and technical skills have been of great value to my clients and to me.

Barbara G. Feinberg

I dedicate this book to my mother,
Ethyl Faye Gottlieb Atkin
*who had the courage to divorce my biological father
and become a single mother in 1939 when I was two and a half years old.
Several years later, she gave me the gift of an extremely positive influence,
Meyer Atkin, my adoptive father,
who knew the meaning of family, parenting and unconditional love.*

Ester Rivkeh Atkin Leutenberg

Our Thanks and Gratitude

To these professionals for their input . . .

Carol Butler, MS Ed, RN, C
Kathy Khalsa, MAJS, OTR/L
Abigail L. Labovitz, MSW, LISW
Matthew I. Feinberg, PhD
Lucy Ritzic, OTR/L
Eileen Regen, M.Ed., CJE
Karal Stern, LISW-S, LICDC-CS
Roberta J. Tonti, LISW-S, IMFT
Fran Zamore, MSW, ACSW

And to these professionals who make us look good!

Publisher and Editorial Director - Carlene Sippola
Art Director – Joy Dey
Editor – Eileen Regen
Proof-reader – Jay Leutenberg

© 2013 WHOLE PERSON ASSOCIATES, 210 WEST MICHIGAN ST., DULUTH MN 55802-1908 ▪ 800-247-6789

The Breakup Experience

Couples become separate entities in the break up and must chart their individual ways.
Loss of a relationship can mean the end of dreams, routines, stability, emotional and financial security, companionship and family as it existed before the breakup. The resulting trauma is one that impacts on the partners, of course. To varying degrees, children, extended family, friends and colleagues suffer from and grieve the loss as well.

In addition to grieving the loss, those in the midst of ending a committed relationship face a great many practical challenges:

- Children
- Parenting
- Housing
- Finances
- Legalities
- Division of property
- Establishing an independent life

The legal break up of couples through divorce adds significantly to the complexity of working through the emotional and practical issues inherent in the process. Divorce involves legal considerations, binding agreements, and an economic reality that can alter the expectations and security of all family members.

Ending a committed relationship is an extended process with different phases. Educating your clients about this progression is an important part of working through the confusing, challenges and difficult experiences of breaking up.

Phases Clients May Encounter

- Significant relationship distress over time
- Increased distance from each other
- Confrontation(s) with partner and family
- Permanent or temporary separation
- Temporary reconciliation
- Decision to end the relationship permanently
- Selection of legal representation in the case of a divorce
- Negotiations for the financial break up
- Creation of a co-parenting plan
- Day by day co-parenting
- Creating a new, single life

Breaking Up is Hard to Do provides activities associated with all of the above phases and challenges of ending a committed relationship.

(Continued on the next page)

The Breakup Experience (Continued)

About Committed Relationships

Breaking Up is Hard to Do addresses issues associated with ending *any* committed arrangement.

A committed relationship in this book is defined as one based on mutually agreed-upon parameters that might involve exclusivity, honesty, openness, loyalty, trust and other implicit and explicit characteristics. Forms of committed relationships can be varied and might be short or long-term. These commitments may be reflected in domestic partnerships, religious and civil unions, single-sex and heterosexual couples living together, "commuter" and other arrangements.

A *divorce* is a legal dissolution of a marriage by a court or other competent body. Many of the same concerns involved in divorce can apply to domestic partners and others in a committed relationship even though resolving legal issues associated with marriage may not be necessary.

Divorce among couples who are married in the eyes of the law is a wide-spread phenomenon in First World countries. Laws governing divorce differ from state to state, and from country to country. Facilitators need to be particularly sensitive to the cultural differences that may have a significant impact on the way in which individuals, families and communities think about and handle divorce.

Format of the Book

Breaking Up is Hard to Do ~ Support for Partners Ending a Committed Relationship is organized to help clients and facilitators with both aspects of breaking up - the process and the practical matters.

- **Section I – The Process**
  This section addresses the emotional impact of breaking up for the partners and their children, if applicable. It provides activities and educational materials to help clients evaluate their committed relationship as objectively as possible, expand coping skills to manage their own and their children's stress and emotional turmoil, develop strategies to get through the aftermath of the break up and begin a new life.

- **Section II – Practical Matters**
  This section focuses on the many external factors that clients may be faced with while simultaneously struggling with complex emotions. It provides concrete exercises to raise awareness of, and useful tips on how to handle the many financial and property-related issues that break ups can raise, particularly in the case of a divorce. Topics include finding advisers and other resources, budgeting, dividing personal property, documenting finances, creating co-parenting agreements, managing the mechanics of divorce and choosing alternative ways to negotiate. Because money is often such a highly charged topic, this section also includes activities to raise awareness of the emotional impact of money and explore ways to learn more about finances.

  Facilitators may feel much more comfortable and better equipped to support clients' emotional experiences. However, both they and their clients may need to become more familiar with the many money and asset-related issues that are also part of ending a committed relationship.

- **Glossary of Terms**
- **Book References**

Using the Book

Breaking Up is Hard to Do ~ Support for Partners Ending a Committed Relationship is designed to facilitate work by mental health professionals, the clergy and any other professionals who support those considering or those in the midst of ending a committed relationship. The book may also be useful in training facilitators who are new to the field.

Because there are so many pages from which to choose, facilitators are encouraged to select the most appropriate ones in each section.

By using the activities in *Breaking Up is Hard to Do*, participants can learn they are not alone and develop important coping strategies. They can find emotional support and practical suggestions, regardless of where they are in this process.

The book's reproducible activity pages can help stimulate conversation, educate, create awareness of what is happening in the present moment, and what might be happening in the future. The activities provide concrete ways for participants to explore each aspect of ending a committed relationship, as well as the associated legal and financial considerations.

The pages can be used in a group, with individuals, as homework assignments, for brainstorming sessions and training purposes. The spiral binding makes it easy to reproduce copies for distribution to participants and trainees. Alternatively, a master copy of any page can be customized as needed.

Each chapter has a separate table of contents with creative tips for the facilitator on how the handouts might be used.

Working with groups:

Helping those going through the possible and actual end of a relationship can be demanding, stimulating, challenging, and ultimately enormously satisfying. Supporting and guiding those dealing with this trauma can make your contribution to the process truly life-changing, both for participants and for you as well.

Groups can be a very dynamic and productive resource for those dealing with the end of a committed relationship. Meeting with others facing the same challenges can be tremendously supportive, educational and reassuring. Knowing that others are dealing with and are surviving the trauma of such a dramatic change in one's life can reduce the participants' sense of isolation and uncertainty and thus significantly enhance their capacity to function and even thrive.

(Continued on the next page)

Using the Book *(Continued)*

How to begin working with groups:

Clarifying how the group will function is recommended as the first step in the group process.

The following guidelines for group participation are important in setting the tone, building and maintaining group cohesion and perhaps most important, making the group a safe place for participants. Distribute the guidelines at the first meeting and keep additional copies available for meetings after that. You and the group may want to add other guidelines as well.

Group Guidelines

- Respect confidentiality – "What happens stays in the group."
- Accept what other participants do and say without criticizing.
- Recognize that members may "pass" and not comment on certain issues.
- Resist offering advice unless the particpant asks for it.
- Focus and support each others' strengths.
- Emphasize the positive.
- Speak from your own experience.
- Be patient with yourself and each other.

You'll notice quotations in the Facilitator Tips for many of the activities.
Reading them aloud to participants can be an effective way to begin those activities.

Before the group begins:

Think about the following questions regarding the group's structure:

- How long will each session last? In part, the length is determined by the number of participants.
- Is this a group participants may join at any time (i.e. an open group)?
- Is this a group participants may join only at the beginning of the process (i.e., a closed group)?.
- Will the group be ongoing or run for a limited number of sessions?
- Are there criteria for participation (age, status of the end of the relationship, gender)?
- Is contact outside of the group by group members encouraged or discouraged?
- Is the group designed to promote discussion or function more like a classroom with the facilitator doing most of the talking?

(Continued on the next page)

Using the Book (Continued)

For each group meeting:
- Begin with a one or two sentence check-in so that members can report on how they're doing and indicate if they need some group time to discuss an issue in more depth.
- Take a moment for everyone to "get present." For example, take three or four deep easy breaths.
- Leave enough time for the activity and discussion.
- If any member seems unable to join in the activities over time, have a private conversation to assess if some individual counseling is in order.
- Alert the group when ten minutes remain in the session.
- Check in with the group in the last five minutes about what stood out for each participant (the "take away").
- Manage the group process so no one participant takes up all the "air time."
- Encourage participation and brain-storming by the group, rather than offering "the answers" yourself unless you see yourself as an "instructor" rather than a facilitator.

Assessment for group participation:
Speaking with a potential participant, either by phone or face-to-face, can provide an opportunity to describe the goals of, and clarify expectations for the group. Participation in a support group is not always the best resource for individuals dealing with the end of a committed relationship. If the group is not suitable, either see the client privately, or refer that individual to appropriate mental health resources.

Think about the following questions to decide if a group is appropriate for a potential participant:
- Is this individual verbal enough to participate in the give-and-take of a group?
- Does this individual appear to have drug or alcohol use issues that could interfere with appropriate participation?
- Are the individual's goals for participation consistent with the group's purpose?
- Is this individual able to function day-to-day, possibly with high levels of stress and upset?
- Can this person adjust his/her schedule to allow for regular attendance?
- Is this individual rational when talking about his/her situation?
- Is the place this person and/or the children live unsafe? *In cases of domestic violence, developing a safety plan is crucial. Referral to an agency focused on domestic violence is appropriate.*
- Does this person talk about **suicide** as an option? *In this case, referral to a mental health expert is critical.*

How to use the book with individuals:
These activity pages can be used in sessions with individuals as well as groups. As clients explore the various issues with which they are dealing, an activity completed during a one-on-one session can educate, focus the conversation, and support clients' explorations of their feelings and options with the counselor.

(Continued on the next page)

Using the Book *(Continued)*

Homework assignments for individual clients and group members:

The activity sheets in this book are useful as homework. Having carefully thought out materials to review at home can enhance clients decision-making, coping skills and facilitate the efficacy in shaping a new life.

Clients are likely to need to gather information, locate documents, and examine financial information outside of counseling sessions. Some of the materials in Section II - Practical Matters are designed as checklists and guides for budgeting, selecting advisers and other aspects of dividing assets and property.

For the Facilitator
Understanding Yourself: The Meaning of *Breaking Up*

The end of a committed relationship can stir up a lot of feelings for you, the facilitator. Depending on your beliefs and personal experience with breakups, you may be coping with strong emotions and opinions that interfere with meeting your clients' needs.

When individuals or couples come for counseling about the decision to separate or stay together, you can be the most helpful if you approach the issue as an open question, even if it appears that one party has definitely decided to leave. Your accepting attitude can give both partners some space to explore the meaning of the end of the committed relationship, recover somewhat from the shock of reaching a crisis point, and begin to see the relationship in a more objective way.

Once the decision to break up is made, you may find yourself reacting emotionally to the many difficult issues your clients face. Your role is to encourage the exploration of the chaotic mixture of feelings and issues swirling around your clients.

As you look through the activities in this book, think about the emotions that are triggered for you by the various topics. Becoming more aware of your own reactions is a helpful starting point for the support and guidance you hope to offer.

Breaking Up Is Hard to Do

TABLE OF CONTENTS

INTRODUCTION	iii–ix

SECTION I – The Process

Chapter 1 – The Future of the Relationship

Chapter Table of Contents and Facilitator Tips	17
Stay or Go?	19–23
Being Left	24
Quality of Current Relationship	25
Our Goals	26
Trying to *Fix* the Relationship	27
My Wants and Needs	28
What Do I Want for Myself?	29–31
What Will Single Life be Like?	32
One Year from Now	33
Clarifying What's Important	34
What is Good and What is Not-So-Good	35
Is a Breakup Right for Me?	36–38
Knowing Myself	39–41
Knowing My Partner	42–43
The BEST and the WORST	44
Thinking about Leaving?	45–46
Prepared to Leave?	47
Staying Safe	48

Chapter 2 – The Emotions of a Breakup

Chapter Table of Contents and Facilitator Tips	49–50
Grieving	51–52
Possible Problems	53–54
What NOT to Expect	55
What is REASONABLE to Expect?	56
Monitoring Moods	57
My Feelings about Anger	58–59
When Do I Over-React?	60
Reducing Anxiety	61
Why Do I Feel this Way?	62
Betrayal	63
Worry Management	64
The Connection between What We Think and What We Feel	65
Emotions Word Search	66
What Were They Thinking?	67
Negative Vibes	68
Positive Supports	69

(Continued on the next page)

TABLE OF CONTENTS *(Continued)*

Chapter 3 – Managing Stress and Thoughts

Chapter Table of Contents and Facilitator Tips 71–72
Relieving Stress: Breathe ... Breathe ... Breathe 73
Guided Imagery 74
Relaxation Techniques 75
Present Moment Awareness 76
Checklist of Enjoyable Activities 77
Coping with "IF ONLY" 78
Journaling 79
I Feel Good That 80
My Regrets 81
Accentuate the Positive 82
Grateful! Seven Days a Week 83
Positive Self-Talk 84
The Message of the Serenity Prayer 85
Saying Hello to New Dreams 86
How Can I Take Care of Myself? 87–88
It's OK to Cry! 89
A MUST - Keeping Your Sense of Humor 90
Positive Affirmations 91

Chapter 4 – Helping the Children through the Breakup

Chapter Table of Contents and Facilitator Tips 93–94
What the Children May Ask 95
Co-Parenting Basics 96
Parenting Issues after a Breakup 97
What to Say? 98
Where Will I Live? 99
I'm Most Worried About 100
We Agree about the Children 101–102
My Goals as a Parent 103
I Expect My Child to 104
Red Flags 105
Different Strokes 106
Impact of a Breakup on Adult Children 107
What Will the Children Think if I Date? 108
Dating When Children are Involved 109
The Twelve Commandments of Co-Parenting 110

(Continued on the next page)

TABLE OF CONTENTS (Continued)

Chapter 5 – Emerging from Divorce

Chapter Table of Contents and Facilitator Tips 111–112
Who am I? Who Am I? I'm _____ 113
My Hopes and Strengths 114
New Opportunities................................... 115
I'm in Charge of Me 116
Just for Me... 117
Routines... 118
Accepting the Past.................................. 119
Letting Go Pointers 120
My New Life.. 121
Single Again.. 122
In the Next Six Months 123
Recovery 124
A Different Family but Still Family 125
Coping with Now.................................... 126
Old and New Traditions 127
It's been a Long Time Since I've Looked for a Job 128
My Own Dreams 129
Rebuild My Social Life 130
Community Resources................................ 131
Dating and the Internet 132

SECTION II: Practical Matters

Chapter 6 – Sensible Steps

Chapter Table of Contents and Facilitator Tips 135
What to Look for in a Legal Advisor.................... 137
What Documents Do I Need? 138
Trust but Verify 139
Structure Your Financial Independence 140
Separation Decisions 141
Who Gets the Sofa? 142
How to REALLY Separate 143
Do I Need a Financial Adviser?........................ 144
Getting Connected 145–146

(Continued on the next page)

TABLE OF CONTENTS (Continued)

Chapter 7 – The Negotiations

Chapter Table of Contents and Facilitator Tips 147
Questions to Ask a Lawyer 149–150
What Can a Lawyer Do for Me? 151
Answers I Need 152–153
Is Mediation Right for Us? 154
Co-Parenting Agreements 155–156
Financial Separation 157
What's it Going to Cost Me? 158
How Long is this Going to Take? 159
What IF? 160

Chapter 8 – Understanding the Financial Divorce

Chapter Table of Contents and Facilitator Tips 161
Prepare for the Financial Divorce 163
My Thoughts about Money 164
Where to Learn More about Money 165
TIPS for Analyzing Options 166
Checklist of Settlement Issues 167

GLOSSARY OF TERMS 169–172
BOOK REFERENCES 173

SECTION I
The Process

SECTION I – **The Process**

CHAPTER **1**–The Future of the Relationship

The Future of the Relationship

Exercises	Facilitator Tips	Page
Stay or Go?	Begin the group asking if they know Kenny Rogers' hit song "The Gambler." Then ask if anyone can recite or sing the first two lines of the refrain: "*You got to know when to hold 'em, know when to fold 'em,* *Know when to walk away and know when to run.*"	19–23
Being Left	This handout raises awareness about feelings. After participants have completed it, ask them to share their responses to the question at the bottom of the page. What surprised them?	24
Quality of Current Relationship	After the handout has been completed, read each item and ask for a show of hands if each item is in their top three feelings. Note the feelings most often felt in the group.	25
Our Goals	After the handout has been completed, ask participants to share whether or not they observed a pattern in their personal responses.	26
Trying to Fix the Relationship	After the handout has been completed, ask participants what they would like to try. Ask group to brainstorm suggestions on how that person might proceed.	27
My Wants and Needs	Prior to distributing the handout, read the following quotation by Ceanne Derohan: *"When you really listen to yourself, you can heal yourself."* Ask participants what the quote means to them.	28
What Do I Want for Myself?	After the handout has been completed, discuss the difference between forgiving and forgetting. Ask for volunteers to share their responses to the last prompt: I want to forgive _____.	29–31
What Will Single Life Be Like?	After participants have completed the handout, invite them to talk about one category that was either exciting or worrysome to them.	32
One Year from Now	Prior to distributing the handout, read the following quotation by Lao-Tzu. *"The journey of a thousand miles begins with a single step."*	33
Clarifying What's Important	After participants have completed the handout, ask them to share the value most important to them. Ask for a volunteer to write the important values on the board, and note the highest values of the group.	34
What is Good and What is Not-So-Good	After participants have completed the handout, ask them to share those in which the good out-weighs the not-so-good and then those in which the not-so-good outweighs the good.	35
Is a Breakup Right for Me?	Write this quotation by Tony Robbins on the board to begin the session. Ask group if they agree with it. *"It is in your moments of decision that your destiny is shaped."*	36–38
Knowing Myself	After participants have completed the handout, ask them to share some realizations that they came to while completing the handout.	39–41
Knowing My Partner	After participants have completed the handout, ask for volunteers to read their responses to the selected questions.	42–43
The BEST and the WORST	Discuss the best-of-the-best and the worst-of-the-worst.	44
Thinking about Leaving	After participants have completed the handout, ask for volunteers to share responses to the last question.	45–46
Prepared to Leave?	After participants have completed the handout, ask for volunteers to share any other suggestions they might have.	47
Staying Safe	Ask participants to complete the handout even if they are not concerned about their safety. Encourage participants to discuss plan in detail.	48

© 2013 WHOLE PEI

SECTION I – The Process

CHAPTER **1–The Future of the Relationship**

Stay or Go?

"You got to know when to hold 'em; know when to fold 'em . . ." ~ Kenny Rogers

Ending a committed relationship is a difficult and emotional decision. As you think about staying or leaving, focus on the impact of your decision for yourself, your partner and your family. Instead of thinking only about breaking up as a yes or no, evaluate the quality of the relationship.

Aspects to consider about your present situation:

Trust – How safe do you feel emotionally? Explain.

_____
_____
_____
_____

Trust – How safe do you feel physically? Explain.

_____
_____
_____
_____

Safety – How safe do you feel sexually? Explain.

_____
_____
_____
_____

Love – Is your love romantic, platonic, intermittent, evaporating, or other? Explain?

_____
_____
_____
_____

Cooperation – How do you help each other with day-to-day responsibilities?

_____
_____
_____
_____

(Continued on the next page)

SECTION I – **The Process**

Stay or Go? (Continued)

Respect – What level of respect does your partner have for you?

_____
_____
_____
_____

Respect – What level of respect do you have for your partner?

_____
_____
_____
_____

Physical intimacy – How are you and your partner "in sync" about intimacy and sex?

_____
_____
_____
_____

Physical intimacy – How are you and your partner not "in sync" about intimacy and sex?

_____
_____
_____
_____

Physical intimacy – How would you describe your sex life? Explain.

_____
_____
_____
_____

Communication – Do you talk to each other about finances? Explain.

_____
_____
_____
_____

(Continued on the next page)

CHAPTER **1–The Future of the Relationship**

Stay or Go? *(Continued)*

Communication – Are you only sharing information or are you able to discuss feelings, worries and excitement?

_____
_____
_____
_____

Values – How much do you agree on ethical and moral issues? How does that influence your relationship?

_____
_____
_____
_____

Religion and spirituality – Describe how you share a religious and/or spiritual belief system. If you do not, describe how that works in your relationship.

_____
_____
_____
_____

Raising children – If you have children, describe how you have or have not been able to find common ground regarding discipline, guidance, medical decisions, educational plans and goals.

_____
_____
_____
_____

Family-of-origin relationships – Do you believe you and/or your partner are more loyal to your own families-of-origin than to each other? Explain.

_____
_____
_____
_____

(Continued on the next page)

SECTION I – The Process

Stay or Go? *(Continued)*

In-Law relationships – How have you or have you not worked out relationships that avoid high levels of conflict with each other's families?

_____
_____
_____
_____

In-Law relationships – Do you have close relationships with your in-laws? Is that likely to continue if your relationship breaks up? Why or why not?

_____
_____
_____
_____

Finances – Are you both contributing to the family economy, either by working outside the home or inside? How does that work for you?

_____
_____
_____
_____

Finances – How do you agree or disagree on methods of spending money? Explain.

_____
_____
_____
_____

Finances – How do you agree or disagree on a budget or saving money? Explain.

_____
_____
_____
_____

Arguing – Do you and your partner stick to the issue at hand when you argue? Explain.

_____
_____
_____
_____

(Continued on the next page)

Stay or Go? *(Continued)*

Arguing – Do you or your partner bring up wrong-doings of the past when arguing? Explain.

_____
_____
_____

Arguing – Does your fighting ever become physical? Describe.

_____
_____
_____
_____

Arguing – When you are arguing with your partner, how safe does everyone in your family feel? Explain.

_____
_____
_____
_____

Future – How do you believe your life (and that of your children, if applicable) would be better without this committed relationship? Explain.

_____
_____
_____
_____

Future – How do you believe your life (and that of your children, if applicable) would be worse without this committed relationship? Explain.

_____
_____
_____
_____
_____
_____

SECTION I – **The Process**

Being Left

The end of a committed relationship is usually difficult. Often the end may come after a long period of distress, uncertainty and frustration for both parties. Sometimes a decision is made by only one partner, and the other partner finds this difficult to cope with. If the end of the commitment seems to come out of nowhere, the sense of rejection can be even more profound. Evaluating the relationship more objectively can help you recognize your own view of the relationship.

Review the following list and check whether the question is true or false for you.

OUR RELATIONSHIP	TRUE	FALSE
Our relationship has been difficult for a long time.		
I have felt I'm running on automatic pilot in my relationship.		
My relationship gives me everything I want.		
I would have left before if I hadn't been so afraid to be on my own.		
I feel as close to my partner as I did when we made a commitment to each other.		
If my partner hadn't been involved in another relationship, everything would be fine.		
This is just a midlife crisis – it'll pass.		
Part of me is relieved that this is finally happening.		
We used to have mostly good times. Now it's mostly bad times.		
With the kids gone, we really just go our own way.		
We probably should never have gotten together in the first place.		
I am still deeply in love with my partner.		
I feel like I'm playing a part in a play, not really being me.		
I knew this was coming – I just didn't want to be the one who broke it up.		
I know we both contributed to the problems we've had.		
This may give me a chance to do some things I couldn't do before.		
I feel my partner has betrayed me.		

Now look at your answers. Which ones surprise you? What have you learned in doing this exercise?

_____

_____

_____

_____

Quality of Current Relationship

When you feel ready to move forward with the process of ending a committed relationship, it is important to assess, as objectively as possible, how daily events are going and how you have been feeling.

Check the emotions you have felt over the past month – always, sometimes or never – and any comments you wish to note.

EMOTIONS	ALWAYS	SOMETIMES	NEVER	COMMENTS
Anxious				
Confident				
Content				
Depressed				
Disappointed				
Empty				
Enraged				
Fearful				
Fulfilled				
Hopeless				
Hurt				
Irritated				
Lonely				
Pleased				
Regretful				
Sad				
Satisfied				
Secure				
Suspicious				
Tense				
Trapped				
OTHER				
OTHER				
OTHER				
OTHER				
OTHER				
OTHER				

What responses surprised you? _____

_____

SECTION I – **The Process**

Our Goals

What are your own personal goals? _____
_____

What are your partner's personal goals? _____
_____

How are these compatible or incompatible with your goals? _____
_____

What are your goals for your family? _____
_____

What are your partner's goals for your family? _____
_____

How are these compatible or incompatible with your goals? _____
_____

What are your career goals? _____
_____

What are your partner's career goals? _____
_____

How are these compatible or incompatible with your goals? _____
_____

What are your leisure goals? _____
_____

What are your partner's leisure goals? _____
_____

How are these compatible or incompatible with your goals? _____
_____

What patterns, if any, do you notice from your responses? _____
_____
_____

CHAPTER **1**–The Future of the Relationship

Trying to *Fix* the Relationship

Usually, one or both partners in a committed relationship have thought about – often for a long time – ending their commitment to each other. Sometimes a particular event, like finding out about an extramarital affair or the death of a loved one, can trigger a decision to divorce. Many individuals, or the couple, make an effort to repair the relationship before making a final decision.

Look at the following list of ways to fix the relationship. Check the ones you've tried, might like to try and those that you do not want to try.

ME	TRIED	MIGHT LIKE TO TRY	DO NOT WANT TO TRY
Couples counseling or group weekend retreat			
Individual counseling			
Talk with a religious or spiritual leader			
Have an honest conversation about the marriage			
Spend or want to spend "quality time" together			
Share the same interests or activities			
Obtain or in treatment for addiction			
Spend time apart			
Talk with a physician about physical concerns			
Discuss problems when they come up			
Support my partner			
Give my partner space			
Talk with trusted friends who share the same challenges			
Temporary separation			
Try reconciliation			

Check responses you believe your partner has tried, might try and does not want to try.

MY PARTNER	TRIED	MIGHT LIKE TO TRY	DO NOT WANT TO TRY
Couples counseling or group weekend retreat			
Individual counseling			
Talk with a religious or spiritual leader			
Have an honest conversation about the marriage			
Spend or want to spend "quality time" together			
Share the same interests or activities			
Obtain or in treatment for addiction			
Spend time apart			
Talk with a physician about physical concerns			
Discuss problems when they come up			
Support my partner			
Give my partner space			
Talk with trusted friends who share the same challenges			
Temporary separation			
Try reconciliation			

© 2013 WHOLE PERSON ASSOCIATES, 210 WEST MICHIGAN ST., DULUTH MN 55802-1908 ▪ 800-247-6789

My Wants and Needs

When facing a life-changing situation, we often think about other people's wants and needs, and how it will affect them. However, recognizing our own wants and needs is a legitimate part of the decision-making process. Fill in your wants and needs.

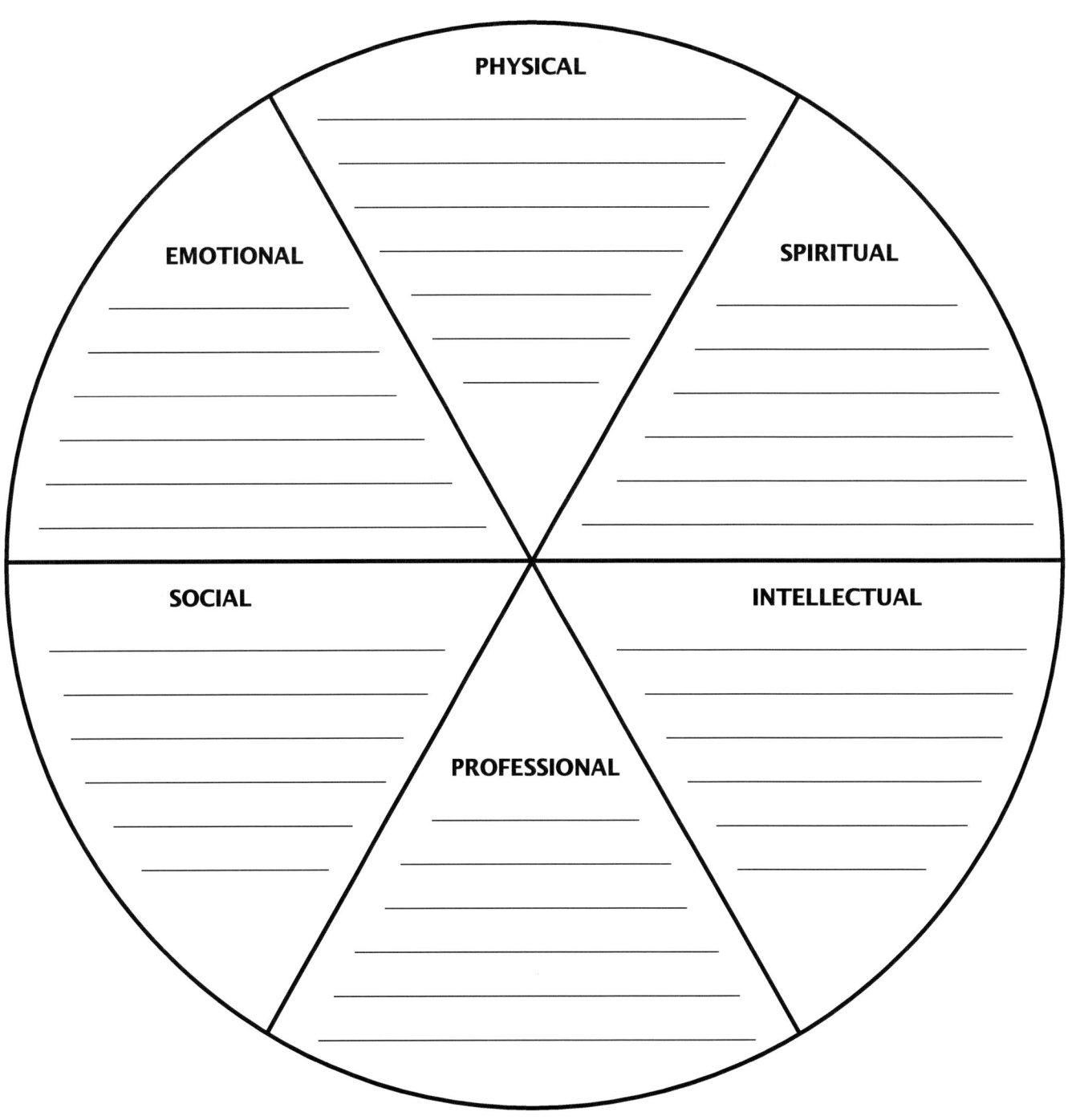

CHAPTER **1—The Future of the Relationship**

What Do I Want for Myself?

A decision about ending a committed relationship depends, in part, on what we want our life to be like in the future.

Finish the following sentences and indicate whether you do or don't have what you want right now. Add some other wants on the blank lines at the end.

I want . . .

a partner who _____

freedom to _____

to learn _____

children _____

shared household responsibilities _____

a healthy life style _____

a partner who shares _____

affection and understanding from _____

a successful career in _____

(Continued on the next page)

SECTION I – **The Process**

What Do I Want for Myself? *(Continued)*

I want . . .

spirituality _____
_____

money to _____
_____

financial security _____
_____

more formal education _____
_____

to live _____
_____

activities that _____
_____

to feel heard by _____
_____

recognition _____
_____

to be free of _____
_____

(Continued on the next page)

CHAPTER **1–The Future of the Relationship**

What Do I Want for Myself? *(Continued)*

I want . . .

to really be myself with _____

_____

to laugh _____

_____

to forget _____

_____

my friends to _____

_____

my family to _____

_____

my home _____

_____

to have fun _____

_____

to look forward to _____

_____

to forgive _____

_____

_____

SECTION I – **The Process**

What Will Single Life Be Like?
Ending a committed relationship requires creating a new life.

In each of the boxes write your visions in 10 words or less of how you envision your life if you are single again. Add your own views in the blank boxes in the last row.
Be as realistic as you can.

HOUSING	WORK	FINANCES
_____	_____	_____
LEISURE ACTIVITIES	**FAMILY LOCATION**	**CHILDREN**
_____	_____	_____
SOCIAL LIFE	**FUN**	**COMMUNITY**
_____	_____	_____
SPIRITUALITY/RELIGION	**PHYSICAL FITNESS**	**SELF-CARE**
_____	_____	_____
WORK-LIFE BALANCE	**EDUCATION**	**INTIMACY**
_____	_____	_____
"A NEW ME"	**TRAVEL**	**VOLUNTEERING**
_____	_____	_____
NEW FRIENDS	**CURRENT FRIENDSHIPS**	**NEW INTERESTS**
_____	_____	_____
_____	_____	_____

CHAPTER **1–The Future of the Relationship**

One Year from Now ...

Although we do not have a crystal ball, trying to imagine what the future could be might provide a road map of where we want to go. Thinking in a positive way can be reassuring and possibly exciting, even though getting from here to there can often seem impossible.

Imagine you are living a happy, fulfilling life one year from now and finish the sentences below:

Professionally, I _____

_____

Socially, I _____

_____

Emotionally, I _____

_____

Physically I _____

_____

Religiously or spiritually, I_____

_____

My family _____

_____

I will have learned _____

_____

My greatest achievement at that point_____

_____

My plans for the five years after that _____

_____

SECTION I – **The Process**

Clarifying What's Important

When going through a breakup, one can lose track of what is really important. The danger is that a person focuses on issues that really do not matter. What does matter – what really makes a difference – can get lost in the process.

VALUES

- Being in charge
- Being part of a couple
- Being secure emotionally
- Being secure financially
- Connection with your extended family
- Control of your own destiny
- Cooperation
- Creating a home
- Fidelity
- Financial freedom
- Having a supportive partner
- Honesty and trustworthiness
- Keeping promises and/or vows
- Living in a peaceful home
- Making decisions independently
- Personal integrity
- Position and/or status in community
- Possessions
- Religious affiliation
- Sense of humor
- Sharing responsibilities equally
- Winning

Identify five values that you hold most dear from the box above.

1. _____
2. _____
3. _____
4. _____
5. _____

Identify five values that are the least important to you from the box above.

1. _____
2. _____
3. _____
4. _____
5. _____

Add any other values that are important to you.

_____ _____
_____ _____
_____ _____

What I value most and why:
_____
_____
_____

What I value least and why:
_____
_____
_____

CHAPTER 1 – The Future of the Relationship

What is Good and What is Not-So-Good?

**Everyone has positive and negative attributes.
List your partner's good and not-so-good attributes.**

GOOD ATTRIBUTES	NOT-SO-GOOD ATTRIBUTES

*Think and talk about whether the goods outweigh the not-so-goods;
or, do the not-so-goods outweigh the goods?*

Do your partner's attributes complement yours?

SECTION I – The Process

Is a Breakup Right for Me?

The decision to break up is an enormous step – highly emotional, anxiety-producing and frightening. If you are struggling to make a decision, the following questions can help you focus on the important aspects of staying in or ending your committed relationship.

1. I value my partner as a person because _____
   _____
   _____

2. How is my life going? Explain. _____
   _____
   _____

3. Am I my real self in this relationship or just going through the motions? Explain. _____
   _____
   _____

4. What are the three most important things I do in my life? _____
   _____
   _____

5. In what ways does my relationship contribute or detract from my successes? _____
   _____
   _____

6. In what ways would a breakup contribute or detract from my successes? _____
   _____
   _____

7. I am most satisfied in my life when _____
   _____
   _____

(Continued on the next page)

# Is a Breakup Right for Me? *(Continued)*

8. I am most dissatisfied in my life when _____
   _____
   _____

9. One year from now I want to be _____
   _____
   _____

10. Is my relationship an excuse for staying "stuck"? Explain. _____
    _____
    _____

11. In what ways will my relationship help or hinder my being where I want to be one year from now?
    _____
    _____
    _____

12. Five years from now I want to be _____
    _____
    _____

13. In what ways will my relationship help or hinder my being where I want to be five years from now? _____
    _____
    _____

14. How are my intimacy needs being met in this relationship? _____
    _____
    _____

15. What is the likelihood that the problems in my relationship can be fixed? Explain. _____
    _____
    _____

(Continued on the next page)

SECTION I – **The Process**

Is a Breakup Right for Me? *(Continued)*

16. If we broke up, my needs _____
_____
_____

17. My relationship would work much better without _____
_____
_____

18. My partner understands (or doesn't understand) how troubled I am in this relationship. Explain.
_____
_____
_____

19. How could I make this relationship work better? _____
_____
_____

20. To make this relationship work, I would need to forgive _____
_____
_____

21. The intimate physical part of my relationship is _____
_____
_____

22. This relationship can work if _____
_____
_____

23. I can see myself growing old with _____
_____
_____

CHAPTER **1–The Future of the Relationship**

Knowing Myself

When we are considering the end of a committed relationship, we often focus more on our partner and forget to look closely at what we're about. *Taking our own pulse* can help us look closely at life in the moment, what we want now and what we want in the future. Thinking about ourselves, and our needs and wants, is part of evaluating whether we think our relationship can be rescued or not. Check one or more box for each statement.

1. **The most difficult part of my life right now:**
   - ❏ I have too much to do and too little time.
   - ❏ Tension in my relationship.
   - ❏ I am depressed most of the time.
   - ❏ I'm lonely.

   Comment _____

2. **What bothers me the most:**
   - ❏ Fear.
   - ❏ Anger.
   - ❏ Having no excitement in my life.
   - ❏ Seeing no hope for the future.
   - ❏ Disappointment.

   Comment _____

3. **The hardest thing for me right now:**
   - ❏ Speaking up for myself.
   - ❏ Recognizing my strengths.
   - ❏ The resentment I have.
   - ❏ Not knowing what's going to happen.

   Comment _____

4. **My life right now:**
   - ❏ Totally chaotic.
   - ❏ The same as it has always been.
   - ❏ Filled with uncertainty.
   - ❏ Suffocating.
   - ❏ Dull and boring.

   Comment _____

(Continued on the next page)

Knowing Myself (Continued)

5. My life would be better:
- ❏ My relationship ended.
- ❏ I had a different boss.
- ❏ We had more money.
- ❏ My kids did what they're told.
- ❏ My children understood what is happening.

Comment _____

6. In the last week, I've enjoyed myself:
- ❏ Never.
- ❏ Once or twice.
- ❏ Every day.
- ❏ Frequently throughout the day.

Comment _____

7. I feel most like myself when I:
- ❏ Am alone.
- ❏ Am with my partner.
- ❏ Spend time with friends.
- ❏ Work.
- ❏ Am with my children.

Comment _____

8. One of the things I fear the most:
- ❏ Being on my own.
- ❏ Feeling trapped.
- ❏ Looking like a failure.
- ❏ Falling apart.
- ❏ Being hated by my children.

Comment _____

9. I want to have more:
- ❏ Self-assurance.
- ❏ Freedom.
- ❏ Control.
- ❏ Affection.

Comment _____

(Continued on the next page)

Knowing Myself (Continued)

10. My partner is:
- ❏ Does the best he/she can.
- ❏ Constantly criticizing me.
- ❏ Never at home.
- ❏ Emotionally unavailable.

Comment _____

11. I want other people to know how:
- ❏ Unhappy I am.
- ❏ Hard I am trying.
- ❏ Much real talent I have.
- ❏ Good a person I am.

Comment _____

12. Ending my relationship means:
- ❏ I am a failure.
- ❏ I will always be alone.
- ❏ I will be able to take charge.
- ❏ my partner won.

Comment _____

13. If our relationship ends, people will think . . .
- ❏ It's my fault.
- ❏ It's my partner's fault.
- ❏ It's not a surprise.
- ❏ It's a shame.

Comment _____

14. If my partner and I separate I will:
- ❏ Be able to handle it.
- ❏ Be totally on my own.
- ❏ Have a lot of support from people I'm close to.
- ❏ Be completely lost.

Comment _____

15. The decision to end my relationship:
- ❏ Is out of my control.
- ❏ Is inevitable.
- ❏ Betrays my values.
- ❏ Might be the best thing after all.

Comment _____

SECTION I – **The Process**

Knowing My Partner

When a relationship is challenged, we are often unable to see our partner's real personality. Finish the sentences below to describe your partner in a comprehensive way.

1. My partner's major strength is _____
   _____

2. When my partner's feelings are hurt, my partner _____
   _____

3. If I ask my partner for help, my partner _____
   _____

4. My partner doesn't seem to understand _____
   _____

5. Since we got together, I believe my partner has changed _____
   _____

6. Other people think my partner _____
   _____

7. What I value most in my partner is _____
   _____

8. What I dislike most in my partner is _____
   _____

9. When it comes to trusting my partner, I _____
   _____

(Continued on the next page)

Knowing My Partner *(Continued)*

10. My partner's loyalty seems to be with _____

11. One important value we both share is _____

12. My partner's behavior with the child(ren) is _____

13. When I have a problem, my partner _____

14. If I need to be comforted, my partner _____

15. I wish my partner were more _____

16. I wish my partner could change _____

17. My hope for my partner is _____

18. I'm afraid my partner will never _____

19. As my partner ages, I expect _____

20. Living with my partner in the future _____

SECTION I – **The Process**

The BEST and the WORST

When we are upset with a relationship, we tend to see only the negative. To have a more objective perspective, it is important to recognize and remember both the best AND the worst parts.

Fill in the blanks for each category and add your own categories at the bottom.

ASPECTS OF RELATIONSHIPS	BEST PARTS ✓ OR X OR WRITE A FEW WORDS TO EXPLAIN	WORST PARTS ✓ OR X OR WRITE A FEW WORDS TO EXPLAIN	N/A
Affection			
Agreement on finances			
Agreement on politics			
Agreement on discipline of children			
Commitment			
Communication of feelings			
Criticism			
Detachment			
Emotional closeness			
Encouragement of each other			
Enjoyment of time together			
Equality of household responsibilities			
Fidelity			
Honesty			
Intimacy			
Kindness			
Optimism about future			
Physical expression of anger			
Physical intimacy			
Relationships with in-laws			
Respect			
Shared goals			
Shared spiritual / religious values			
Shared values			
Socializing			
Support of professional ambitions			
Teamwork			
Trust			

CHAPTER **1 – The Future of the Relationship**

Thinking about Leaving?

Most people considering a breakup have been thinking about it for a long time and many issues come into play. These questions may help you focus on what you're thinking about right now.

What made you think seriously about ending your relationship now? _____
_____
_____

When you and your partner are alone together ...

- How do you feel about yourself? _____
_____
_____

- How do you feel about your partner? _____
_____
_____

When you and your partner are with your family ...

- How do you feel about yourself? _____
_____
_____

- How do you feel about your partner? _____
_____
_____

When you and your partner are trying to solve a problem ...

- How do you feel about yourself? _____
_____
_____

- How do you feel about your partner? _____
_____
_____

When you and your partner are in social situations (with friends, co-workers, etc.) ...

- How do you feel about yourself? _____
_____
_____

- How do you feel about your partner? _____
_____
_____

(Continued on the next page)

SECTION I – **The Process**

Thinking about Leaving? *(Continued)*

When you are alone …

- How do you feel about yourself? _____
  _____
  _____

- How do you feel about your partner? _____
  _____
  _____

When you are worried …

- How do you feel about yourself? _____
  _____
  _____

- How do you feel about your partner? _____
  _____
  _____

When do you feel the most content?

- Is your partner present at that time? _____
  _____
  _____

When is your self-esteem at its best?

- Is your partner present at that time? _____
  _____
  _____

When is your energy level at its highest?

- Is your partner present at that time? _____
  _____
  _____

In what ways do you still respect your partner? _____
_____
_____

Prepared to Leave?

Prepare and hide this information in a safe place if you can:

- ❑ Bank account(s) information
- ❑ Your own checking account (if you don't have one, apply for your own)
- ❑ Blank checks
- ❑ Cash
- ❑ Your own credit card (if you don't have one, apply for your own)
- ❑ A list of phone numbers of medical people
- ❑ A list of phone numbers of trusted family and friends
- ❑ An extra set of car keys hidden in a place where you can grab them easily.
- ❑ A bag hidden with things you and the children will need in an emergency.
- ❑ List or duplicate copies of all prescriptions
- ❑ Duplicates of all medicines for you and the children
- ❑ Copies of important papers
    - Birth certificates
    - Car registration
    - Proof of medical and car insurance
    - Welfare identification
    - School records
    - Driver's license
    - Passports
    - Green cards
    - Work permits
    - Restraining order from court
    - _____
    - _____
    - _____
    - _____
    - _____

Keep your cell phone charged.

Think about getting a separate cell phone just for emergencies.

SECTION I – **The Process**

Staying Safe

Keeping yourself and your children safe is the most important issue when you're thinking about ending a committed relationship. Having a safety plan is critical if your relationship has included, or might include physical, verbal and/or psychological abuse. Part of being safe is being prepared to go to a safe haven at a moment's notice.

This checklist will help you be ready to leave if you must.

Add some other items that are important in your personal situation.

- ❏ Important phone number list, including police, hotlines, friends and a local shelter.

- ❏ Neighbors you can tell about your concerns. Ask them to call the police if they hear angry or violent noises.

- ❏ Change the password on your computer.

- ❏ A few trusted people whom you can call to help you.

- ❏ Teach your children to call 911.

- ❏ Make up a code word you can use with your children, friends and neighbors if you are in danger.

- ❏ Practice ways to get out of the house quickly with your children - for example, have the kids help you take out the trash, go to the store, walk the dog, visit a neighbor.

- ❏ Identify a safer place in your house to go if you feel in danger. Choose a place with an exit and where there are no guns if possible.

- ❏ If you need to leave the house, time it to leave when your partner is not at home.

- ❏ If there are guns in the house, try to find a way to get them out of the house.

- ❏ Think about where you would go, even if you don't think you'll actually need to leave.

- ❏ Open a bank account and credit card in your own name.

- ❏ Open your own safety deposit box and put valuables in it.

- ❏ Review your safety plan often, and revise if needed.

- ❏ _____

- ❏ _____

- ❏ _____

CHAPTER 2–**The Emotions of a Breakup**

The Emotions of a Breakup

Exercises	Facilitator Tips	Page
Grieving	Distribute the first page of the handout. Read aloud or ask participants to share in the reading of the first page. Emphasize to participants that in the process of grieving, they may go back and forth between the four steps of grieving. Then distribute the second page and ask participants to complete the handout.	51–52
Possible Problems	Before distributing the three-page handout, write this quotation on the board: *"It's not a problem until it's your problem."* ~ Marty Boxerhorn Encourage discussion of the quotation. After participants have completed the pages, ask for volunteers to share their most challenging problem and their possible solution. Others might have suggestions, also.	53–54

What NOT to Expect	Read and discuss this quotation prior to distributing the handout:
	    "Blessed is he who expects nothing, for he shall never be disappointed."
	              ~Alexander Pope
	Encourage discussion of the quotation first and then distribute the handout.
		55

What is REASONABLE to Expect	After participants have completed the handout, ask volunteers to share any other items they filled In at the bottom of the page.	56
Monitoring Moods	Notice if any of the participants have checked many of the items. It may be appropriate to suggest they receive further mental health counseling.	57
My Feelings about Anger	After the handout has been completed, ask for a show of hands, true or false, of each item. As you see a wide disparity on items, group members can brainstorm their thoughts.	58–59
When Do I Over-React?	After participants have completed the handout: Read the following quotation aloud by The Buddha: *"Holding on to anger is like grasping a hot coal with the intent of throwing it at someone else; you are the one who gets burned."* Ask participants what the quote means to them. Ask for volunteers to share one of their overreactions.	60
Reducing Anxiety	Read the top section up to Physical Tension. Ask for three volunteers to each read one of the sections: Physical Tension, Anxious Thoughts and Stop Distressing Thoughts. After each section is read, ask the participants to name the actions they are most interested in taking and why.	61
Why Do I Feel This Way?	After participants have completed the handout: Ask: *Are there times that you are feeling more than one emotion at the same time?* An example might be papers are signed ending the committed relationship. Feelings of relief, fear, regret and happiness can happen all at the same time. Ask them to share their own examples.	62
Betrayal	If participants have been betrayed by more than one person, photocopy enough handouts for them to complete one about each person who betrayed them.	63
Worry Management	As an alternative to using this as a handout, photocopy as many as needed and cut boxes apart. Distribute one box to each participant. The participants write one of their own worries on the first line. They fold them in half and put them in a hat or container. Each participant picks one and writes a response to the prompt: *I can handle this issue by___.* After the response is finished, papers can go back in the hat or container. Each participant picks one and reads it. As each is read aloud, the group can discuss and brainstorm.	64

(Continued on the next page)

© 2013 WHOLE PERSON ASSOCIATES, 210 WEST MICHIGAN ST., DULUTH MN 55802-1908 ▪ 800-247-6789

SECTION I – **The Process**

The Emotions of a Breakup *(Continued)*

Exercises	Facilitator Tips	Page
The Connection between What We Think and What We Feel	After completing the handout, ask participants if they would be willing to share one of their responses.	65
Emotions Word Search	Prior to beginning the Emotions Word Search, inform participants that the words are forward and diagonal. After participants have completed the handout, ask a volunteer to read the emotions words at the bottom and ask for a show of hands after each emotion is read as to whether they have felt this emotion in the past week.	66
What Were They Thinking?	Prior to distributing handouts, remind participants that they are not alone – people often say insensitive or hurtful things. After participants have completed the handout, ask them to relate any other comments made to them that were hurtful. Brainstorm possible responses to selected statements in the handout that were checked or to those comments that participants mentioned were said to them.	67
Negative Vibes	Begin the session with this Louisa Mae Alcott quotation, *"Good books, like good friends, are few and chosen."* Ask for a show of hands from the participants if they have any friends who, at this point in their lives, pull them down, de-energize them or make them feel worse when they are with them. Distribute the handout.	68
Positive Supports	Begin the session with Herbert Humphrey's quotation, *"The greatest healing therapy is friendship and love."* After distributing the handout, ask participants to place a check in one or more of the last four columns as to the best way to contact each particular person. When handouts are completed, ask participants to count the total amount of people that they listed. Explain that the more people they have listed the better. This avoids burnout by individuals; if someone's unavailable, there are others to call, etc. If they only have a few names, suggest that this may be the time to broaden their support base.	69

Grieving

The end of a committed relationship is an enormous loss whether you initiated the process, or are struggling to accept your partner's decision. Initially, you might feel shock that this is actually happening, or relief that the situation has finally come to a head.

Nonetheless, we grieve this loss in much the same way that we respond to a death and other losses. In this case, the pain of the loss is about the end of a way of life, the dreams we might have had and the future we are facing.

Once the shock and possibly relief have subsided, we begin to grieve. Experts explain that grieving is a predictable process, but keep in mind this is not a "first step, second step" process. Over time, we may go back and forth from one to another.

1. **ACCEPT THE LOSS** – Here is where we begin to grieve. We may lose hope that the end of the relationship is reversible and intellectually recognize that the end of the relationship as we knew it is inevitable, and, in fact, already underway.

2. **FEEL THE FEELINGS** – We can be flooded with different and often contrary feelings at this stage of grieving. While we may want to push those feelings away, we need to begin to recognize, name and acknowledge the many emotions we experience. Your way of coping is unique and appropriate for you. Nonetheless, exploring your feelings here in a safe environment can reduce the pressure that builds up when you try to suppress them.

3. **ADJUST** – In this phase, we begin to reorganize our lives and acknowledge that life must go on. We may move furniture, reach out to old and new friends as a single person and try to pay extra attention to our children who are grieving as well. Ever so gradually, our lives start to have a different shape and routine. While we are still likely to have confusing feelings, our behavior and attitude does change.

4. **MOVE FORWARD** – This last phase is the time when we take charge of our lives more actively – we recognize we have grown through this difficult time. While still being challenged by distressing feelings, we start to see ourselves in a different way:

    "We have broken-up. We are not in the process of breaking-up."

Our definition of "ourselves" broadens to recognize other aspects of who we are.
We still may feel a sense of loss and sadness, but in different ways from before.

(Continued on the next page)

SECTION I – **The Process**

Grieving (Continued)

ACCEPT THE LOSS

Accepting the loss means recognizing it intellectually. Talking about the breakup is the beginning of grief. One difficult task is finding words to tell family and friends that you and your partner are breaking-up. Write a sentence (with which you will feel comfortable) that you might use when you tell people.

_____
_____
_____
_____
_____

FEEL THE FEELINGS

Your emotions during this process are likely to be overwhelming at times, possibly surprising and very intense. List three feelings you've had that are the most difficult for you to handle.

1. _____
2. _____
3. _____

ADJUST

As you learn to live with the loss or your relationship, you'll have many decisions to make, many of which you'll make on your own. List the three decisions and possible outcomes you're facing that will help you adjust to the break-up.

1. _____
2. _____
3. _____

MOVE FORWARD

It takes a long time to feel settled in your new life and to know yourself in a different way. List three ways you'll know you're moving forward.

1. _____
2. _____
3. _____

CHAPTER **2**–The Emotions of a Breakup

Possible Problems

People have compared ending a committed relationship to riding a roller coaster and a sailboat in rough water, both at the same time. As you move toward finalizing the formal or legal aspect of your breakup, you need to be aware of some possible pitfalls. Read these potential problems and write possible solutions as they apply to you.

POSSIBLE PROBLEM: Guilt

Because you feel guilty, you might not negotiate for what is appropriate and reasonable based on financial data and the law.

Possible solution: _____

_____

_____

_____

POSSIBLE PROBLEM: Relying on your partner to make financial decisions.

You and your partner are likely to have different goals and competing interests in the division of your assets. So your partner's decisions might not be best for you.

Possible solution: _____

_____

_____

_____

POSSIBLE PROBLEM: Having the same lawyer represent both of you.

Using the same lawyer might be less expensive, but unless the lawyer is mediating your divorce settlement, your best interests may not always be the lawyer's priority.

Possible solution: _____

_____

_____

(Continued on the next page)

Possible Problems *(Continued)*

POSSIBLE PROBLEM: Settling too quickly

Negotiations can be extremely stressful. You may be so eager to finalize the divorce, that you don't press to get a settlement, which would leave you in as secure a position in the future as possible. You should be aware that you just could be delaying problems that you will have to face later.

Possible solution: _____

_____

_____

_____

POSSIBLE PROBLEM: Giving up

You may feel unable to understand all the ins and outs of a breakup so you just agree to anything and everything your partner or lawyer suggests.

Possible solution: _____

_____

_____

_____

POSSIBLE PROBLEM: Thinking in the short-term

The financial decisions you make now may have a significant impact on your future in five years, ten years or into retirement.

Possible solution: _____

_____

_____

_____

What NOT to Expect

Sometimes when partners have separated, they have unrealistic expectations of themselves and others. Having hopes about how things might go can give partners a sense of direction. However, relying on those hopes to make things better can lessen the control they have over their lives.

Check unrealistic expectations in this list and recognize as unlikely. Add others you might have.

- ❏ Regular baby-sitting from family
- ❏ Children always behaving well
- ❏ Feeling of serenity
- ❏ Knowing what to do all the time
- ❏ Ability to figure out solutions easily
- ❏ Life going on unchanged
- ❏ Constant civility with your ex
- ❏ Help from your ex around the house
- ❏ Same level of productivity at work
- ❏ Economic stability
- ❏ Unchanged social relationships
- ❏ Life running smoothly
- ❏ Stable moods
- ❏ Continuing close relationships with in-laws
- ❏ Unimpaired self-esteem
- ❏ Unchanged friendships
- ❏ Feelings of self-assurance at all times
- ❏ Having no regrets
- ❏ _____
- ❏ _____
- ❏ _____
- ❏ _____

SECTION I – **The Process**

What is REASONABLE to Expect

There are some things in a break up that are reasonable to expect. Check those that you have already become aware of or anticipate. Add your own at the bottom.

- ❏ A mixture of reactions from everyone
- ❏ Anger
- ❏ Children's confusion, anger, sadness
- ❏ Concern about finances
- ❏ Control over your own future
- ❏ Doubting yourself
- ❏ Feelings of anxiety
- ❏ Feelings of guilt
- ❏ Finding some things that the partner did and you have no idea what to do
- ❏ Friendly, or at least civil conversations when it comes to the children
- ❏ Friends or relatives whom you can call on to help problem-solve
- ❏ Friends who let you down
- ❏ Friends who step up to the plate
- ❏ Life to be very different, some things positive and some not
- ❏ Moodiness
- ❏ Mourning the loss of the family as it was
- ❏ Needing more help than you thought you would
- ❏ New relationships with partners' family
- ❏ Positive and negative aspects of being single
- ❏ Possibly being more distracted at work
- ❏ _____
- ❏ _____
- ❏ _____
- ❏ _____

CHAPTER 2—The Emotions of a Breakup

Monitoring Moods

Mood swings are very common during times of great stress, like a breakup.
Keeping an eye on your moods can help you avoid feeling so down, or so up, that you aren't able to function well. It will also allow you to be an easier person to be around.

Check in with yourself once a week to see how you're doing.

MOODS	WEEK 1	WEEK 2	WEEK 3	WEEK 4
Angry outbursts				
Constant irritability				
Continual state of excitement				
Crying spells				
Dangerous behaviors				
Disinterest in pleasurable activities				
Disrupted sleep				
Emotional numbness				
Excessive guilt feelings				
Feelings of helplessness				
Feelings of hopelessness				
High anxiety				
Inability to make decisions				
Irresponsible behavior				
Lack of motivation				
Making unrealistic plans and goals				
Memory problems				
Panic attacks				
Periods of intense irritability				
Poor concentration				
Procrastination				
Sexual acting out				
Thoughts of suicide				
Unceasing energy and activity				
Uncommonly happy mood				
Uncontrolled spending				
Unhealthy risk-taking				
Unintended increase or decrease in weight				
Unusual bursts of enthusiasm				

© 2013 WHOLE PERSON ASSOCIATES, 210 WEST MICHIGAN ST., DULUTH MN 55802-1908 ▪ 800-247-6789

SECTION I – The Process

My Feelings about Anger

Feeling angry – sometimes furious – during and after a breakup is common. Understanding and managing that anger gives you more of a sense of control.

**Respond by circling whether each item is true or false for YOU and explain why.
(T = True, F = False)**

1. Blowing off steam is healthy. T F _____
   _____
   _____

2. Holding anger in is always unhealthy. T F _____
   _____
   _____

3. Becoming angry is the only way I can get people to listen to me. T F ____
   _____
   _____

4. Other people make me angry. It's their fault. T F _____
   _____
   _____

5. Anger is a feeling I can control. T F _____
   _____
   _____

6. The only way I can manage my anger is to push it down. T F _____
   _____
   _____

(Continued on the next page)

My Feelings about Anger *(Continued)*

7. The best way for me to respond when someone gets angry is to get angry right back. T   F
   _____
   _____

8. Men are allowed to get angry. Women are not! T   F _____
   _____
   _____

9. Being assertive is the same thing as being aggressive. T   F _____
   _____
   _____

10. A good motto is "Don't get mad. Get even." T   F _____
    _____
    _____

11. Out-of-control anger can be hurtful to my health. T   F _____
    _____
    _____

12. Becoming very angry and getting over it quickly is okay. T   F _____
    _____
    _____

13. I don't know what triggers my anger. T   F _____
    _____
    _____

14. The past has nothing to do with why I get angry. T   F _____
    _____
    _____

SECTION I – **The Process**

When Do I Over-React?

We can be surprised by a very strong reaction to what later seems like a very small thing. Often, it is an over-reaction. Later we may regret what we said or did. Our intense response may be triggered by something from the past without our even being aware of it. If we understand what triggers our reactions, we may be able to avoid what we later realize were unnecessary confrontations.

List the people, situations and words that angered you this past week.
Then, write what might have triggered your reaction.

- -

In this past week, I over-reacted _____
_____
_____ .

The same type of thing used to happen when _____
_____
_____ .

- -

In this past week, I over-reacted _____
_____
_____ .

The same type of thing used to happen when _____
_____
_____ .

- -

In this past week, I over-reacted _____
_____
_____ .

The same type of thing used to happen when _____
_____
_____ .

- -

Reducing Anxiety

Feeling anxious and worried much of the time is a common response to an emotional crisis like a breakup. Sometimes we feel so anxious that we can't take any action.

> **Anxiety can take three forms:**
> - **physical tension**
> - **anxious and worrisome thoughts with feelings of doom**
> - **constant distressful thoughts**

Physical Tension: Muscles stiffening up, teeth grinding, rapid heartbeat, jitteriness, tight chest or belly. Suggestions:

- Reduce or eliminate caffeine, alcohol, tobacco, sugar or unnatural sweeteners.
- Exercise.
- Use stress reduction techniques.
- Learn present moment awareness exercises.
- Take deep breaths.
- Listen to guided imagery and other relaxation CDs.

Anxious Thoughts: Thoughts that dwell on regrets from the past and worries about the future. Suggestions:

- Say to yourself, "Oh, it's only me being anxious again." Or "My anxious brain is firing up again."
- Set up a specific worry-time – 15 minutes to worry – and then no more that day.
- Say STOP every single time you worry other than your worry-time.
- Say to yourself, "I'll worry during my worry time."
- Repeat this mantra often, "I'm okay," "I don't need to worry."
- Refusing to face anger creates anxiety. Say to yourself, "If I were angry, I'd be angry about …"

Stop Distressing Thoughts:
Suggestions:

- Put concerns in a jar and put jar on shelf (visualization).
- Invite a peaceful thought in (meditation).
- Exercise.
- Plan instead of worrying. Identify specific problem; list options to solve problem; pick one option; write a plan of action.
- Communicate and express distressing thoughts for 5-10 minutes with a good, trusted friend and then move on. Show interest and care about that friend's issues.

> *Remember: Breathing deeply and calmly throughout the day is essential to reducing anxiety.*

SECTION I – **The Process**

Why Do I Feel This Way?

Everyone deals with a breakup in a way that's unique and personal. One thing is for sure, this process stirs up a lot of different and opposite emotions (often at the same time). Understanding what triggers particular feelings can help you tolerate them better.

Check the feelings you have had in the last little while and try to identify what triggered each feeling.

FEELINGS	TRIGGERED BY
Abandoned	
Angry	
Ashamed	
Bitter	
Confused	
Disconnected	
Disheartened	
Ecstatic	
Embarrassed	
Empty	
Euphoric	
Free	
Frightened	
Guilty	
Helpless	
Hopeless	
Isolated	
Joyless	
Lonely	
Numb	
Regretful	
Relieved	
Shocked	
Stuck	
Traumatized	
Uncertain	
Other	

CHAPTER **2–The Emotions of a Breakup**

Betrayal

A sense of betrayal is often an intense emotion in the face of a breakup. While betrayal in a committed relationship by a partner is devastating, betrayals by others can also be terribly upsetting. Although you can't read anyone's mind to understand what motivated the betrayal, you can identify the nature of your own pain.

The person who betrayed me was _____
NAME OR INITIALS

Check the betrayals you've experienced and write a few words that express your feelings. Skip the items that do not apply.

- ❏ Abuses me and/or my children physically, emotionally, sexually or verbally _____
- ❏ Acts disloyally _____
- ❏ Avoids me _____
- ❏ Blames me for the end of the relationship _____
- ❏ Breaks promises _____
- ❏ Continues addictive behavior _____
- ❏ Criticizes my decisions _____
- ❏ Demonstrates no sensitivity to my needs _____
- ❏ Disapproves of my parenting style _____
- ❏ Insists on rigid work hours _____
- ❏ Keeps secrets _____
- ❏ Lies _____
- ❏ Limits availability _____
- ❏ Maintains a secret life _____
- ❏ Makes improper advances and/or has inappropriate expectations _____
- ❏ Neglects me _____
- ❏ No longer cares about me _____
- ❏ Offers no support _____
- ❏ Passes judgment on my religious or spiritual beliefs _____
- ❏ Piles more work on me at the office _____
- ❏ Refuses to help in an emergency _____
- ❏ Shows no interest in my situation _____
- ❏ Speaks and acts disrespectfully _____
- ❏ Takes my partner's side _____
- ❏ Talks about me behind my back _____
- ❏ Violates my trust _____
- ❏ Withholds affection _____
- ❏ Other _____
- ❏ Other _____

SECTION I – The Process

Worry Management

Going through a breakup creates an enormous amount of anxiety and worry because of having to face so many unknowns. When you identify your biggest worries, you can begin to look at the issues more objectively and then plan more effectively.

List four items you have worried about in the past week and then comment on how you might handle the issue.

1. _____

   I can handle this issue by _____
   _____
   _____
   _____

2. _____

   I can handle this issue by _____
   _____
   _____
   _____

3. _____

   I can handle this issue by _____
   _____
   _____
   _____

4. _____

   I can handle this issue by _____
   _____
   _____
   _____

The Connection between What We Think and What We Feel

We usually think we feel a certain way because of what has happened – perhaps an event or another person that *makes* us feel sad, happy, angry, frustrated, scared or any other emotion. In fact, no one can *make* us feel anything. Emotions are not so much caused by something or someone else. Actually, how people *interpret and think what happened* are really the cause of whatever they feel. If people have negative thoughts and ways of seeing the world, themselves and the future, they will have unpleasant reactions, and feel angry, hurt, etc.

Many people routinely think in negative ways without even recognizing they're doing it.

Five of the most common negative thought patterns:

1. ***Shoulds* and *musts* for ourselves and others:** When we think rules must be obeyed all the time by everyone including ourselves, we get frustrated and angry when the rules aren't being followed. Describe a time and what thoughts went through your mind when one of your rules wasn't being followed. _____

_____

How did you feel at that time? _____

2. **Mind reading:** Describe a time and what thoughts went through your mind when you were positive you knew what that other person was thinking or feeling without being told? _____

_____

How did you feel at that time? _____

3. **Blaming other people or situations:** Describe a time and what thoughts went through your mind when you blamed someone or something else for a mistake or problem? _____

_____

How did you feel at that time? _____

4. **Overgeneralizing:** Describe a time and what thoughts went through your mind when you or someone else used the words always, never, or everyone thinks in a negative way? _____

_____

How did you feel at that time? _____

5. **Fortune Telling:** Describe a time and what thoughts went through your mind when you just knew that something would work out badly? _____

_____

How did you feel when you thought that? _____

SECTION I – The Process

Emotions Word Search

Circle the thirty *emotional* words, common to people in a breakup.

Z	S	M	B	U	D	Q	W	E	R	K	T	J	Y	H	U	G	I	F	O	S	P	T	A	P
L	O	N	L	M	B	C	V	X	Z	A	K	E	D	E	T	E	R	M	I	N	E	D	R	E
G	R	E	A	T	O	V	E	R	W	H	E	L	M	E	D	Y	E	L	O	B	L	U	W	A
T	R	I	M	R	A	T	O	N	G	A	T	I	N	F	S	T	A	I	L	H	O	U	R	C
C	Y	Q	E	Z	E	O	B	K	L	O	L	K	A	D	V	E	T	M	L	U	S	R	M	E
F	H	O	I	U	D	D	E	T	E	R	M	I	N	E	D	S	D	E	S	P	A	I	R	F
B	I	U	Z	C	I	E	T	P	O	I	T	R	E	X	U	C	S	T	M	P	O	M	S	U
R	A	L	P	A	I	N	O	J	H	E	F	P	E	A	B	A	P	L	Y	F	E	P	S	L
A	C	V	I	B	R	I	N	D	L	E	S	T	H	B	R	I	O	R	E	M	O	A	U	I
S	O	R	T	L	R	A	G	E	B	O	N	X	C	E	R	T	I	E	S	L	A	T	E	N
P	N	K	I	O	S	L	N	A	O	R	E	N	A	F	I	S	U	S	P	I	C	I	O	N
O	F	F	C	T	E	X	A	G	R	I	E	F	L	R	V	A	R	E	I	T	Y	E	N	D
O	U	R	B	R	A	N	F	O	D	M	C	E	R	U	T	E	A	N	E	E	S	N	A	K
D	S	I	O	V	B	I	T	T	E	R	N	E	S	S	C	R	A	T	E	R	N	C	M	N
B	I	V	C	X	Z	A	S	D	F	G	H	C	J	T	S	C	E	M	O	Y	L	E	O	B
N	O	S	H	O	C	K	T	R	E	M	A	A	I	R	E	L	I	E	F	V	E	R	I	B
A	N	B	A	Y	F	O	G	G	L	R	U	N	B	A	T	O	N	N	E	R	S	E	L	L
M	I	O	N	P	A	D	R	A	E	J	A	Y	X	T	K	S	A	T	H	Y	S	I	R	I
L	Y	N	G	N	P	E	A	D	M	Y	M	I	T	I	C	S	H	E	L	L	A	G	L	T
E	R	J	E	A	C	K	D	A	V	I	Y	U	D	O	E	L	D	I	S	T	R	U	S	T
A	R	I	R	P	A	N	I	C	J	E	N	N	Y	N	S	T	O	P	H	I	A	I	N	I
C	K	M	L	K	A	S	O	N	T	J	E	A	L	O	U	S	Y	Y	D	L	E	L	R	K
Y	L	E	E	V	B	R	A	N	T	M	O	S	A	V	D	A	S	H	A	I	N	T	A	N
E	L	L	E	S	D	R	E	G	R	E	T	M	B	C	Z	L	J	G	D	A	P	I	Y	R
W	N	V	X	L	K	J	H	G	F	E	D	D	S	P	O	U	T	E	Q	W	E	Y	O	U

Check the emotions you have felt in the last week:

- ❏ ANGER
- ❏ ANXIETY
- ❏ BITTERNESS
- ❏ BLAME
- ❏ CONFUSION
- ❏ DENIAL
- ❏ DESPAIR
- ❏ DETERMINED
- ❏ DISAPPOINTED
- ❏ DISTRUST

- ❏ EXHAUSTION
- ❏ FRUSTRATION
- ❏ GRIEF
- ❏ GUILT
- ❏ IMPATIENCE
- ❏ JEALOUSY
- ❏ LOSS
- ❏ OVERWHELMED
- ❏ PAIN
- ❏ PANIC

- ❏ PEACEFUL
- ❏ RAGE
- ❏ REGRET
- ❏ RELIEF
- ❏ RESENTMENT
- ❏ SAD
- ❏ SCARED
- ❏ SHOCK
- ❏ SORRY
- ❏ SUSPICION

CHAPTER 2–The Emotions of a Breakup

What Were They Thinking?

Some people say the first thing on their minds when finding out someone has broken up. They may mean well, they may not know the right thing to say, or they might not be very sensitive, but in all cases, their comments can hurt.

Check any of the comments that have been said to you:

- ❏ Aha! I knew you were not a good match!
- ❏ Are you sure?
- ❏ At least you didn't have children.
- ❏ But she has such a nice family.
- ❏ Couldn't you have prevented it?
- ❏ Did you make out well with the settlement?
- ❏ Did you try hard enough?
- ❏ He seemed like such a nice guy.
- ❏ How are you going to manage alone?
- ❏ How can you do that to the children?
- ❏ I didn't like her anyway.
- ❏ I don't believe in divorce.
- ❏ I hope you walk away with a lot of money.
- ❏ I know exactly how you feel.
- ❏ I never could understand what you saw in him.
- ❏ I saw it coming all along!
- ❏ I'm sure you just want to be left alone.
- ❏ It's about time!
- ❏ Oh, you're attractive. You won't be alone for long.
- ❏ She seemed like such a lovely woman.
- ❏ Well, everything happens for a reason.
- ❏ What happened?
- ❏ Whose fault was it?
- ❏ Why didn't you tell me?
- ❏ Why?
- ❏ Why? You have such a perfect life.
- ❏ _____
- ❏ _____

It might be helpful for you to have a few prepared responses.
- Things have changed.
- I'm not ready to talk about it.
- We have decided to split up.
- _____
- _____
- _____
- _____

SECTION I – The Process

Negative Vibes

Some of our relationships can be draining, demanding and insensitive. When we are dealing with a break up, the negativity we experience in our dealings with such people is particularly difficult and damaging. Because we need all our energy to deal with the challenges in our lives, we may need to get some distance from those negative people, if not permanently, at least for now.

Fill in the name of those people who fit the description in the Negative Vibes column below. It is okay to repeat the people if they fit into different situations. You can use initials to save space. Try to be objective in your assessment of how the relationship works for you. In the last column, write how you might avoid regular contact with those who give out negative vibes, at least temporarily.

Negative Vibes	Who? (Can be more than one person)	How I Can Limit Contact
Acts like a know-it-all		
Advises me when I don't ask		
Assumes I'm inadequate		
Avoids just "hanging out" with me		
Blames me for the breakup		
Bores me		
Breaks dates		
Can't empathize with my situation		
Does not see my point of view		
Criticizes me		
Discourages me		
Doesn't seem to really hear me		
Does not suggest solutions to problems		
Gives me more tasks to do		
Has a need to "win" any conversation		
Hesitates to make time for me		
Ignores my religious/spiritual beliefs		
Is self-centered		
Isn't there for me in an emergency		
Judges me		
Misunderstands my family dynamics		
No longer invites me to parties		
Opposes my suggestions		
Preaches at me		
Predicts a terrible future for me		
Refuses to talk to me		
Rejects my feelings		
Saps my energy		
Says I'm ruining my children's lives		
Sees only the negative in any situation		
Takes my ex's side		
Tiptoes around me		
Turns me down to try something new		
Will not listen to me		
Won't adjust to my schedule		

CHAPTER 2 – The Emotions of a Breakup

Positive Supports

**Family members and friends can be great supports – however – no one person can meet ALL of our needs and everyone is not always available when needed. Below, fill in the people in your life who are positive influences and place a check in the columns of ways you can contact them. You may repeat the people if they fit into different situations.
Try to involve as many people as possible.**

Situation	Who? (Can be more than one person)	Email	Phone	Get together	Other
Accepts me for who I am					
Allows me to cry					
Always willing to try something new					
Appreciates a fun time					
Available for a late evening talk					
Believes in my future					
Cares about my children					
Encourages me					
Energizes me					
Enjoys walking and talking					
Finds ways to help me to laugh					
Gives me good advice					
Goes shopping					
Hears me without trying to 'fix' me					
Helps me with things to do in the house					
Invites me out for breakfast					
Is aware of my family dynamics					
Is non-judgmental					
Is very reassuring					
Is willing to tell me 'like it is'					
Keeps me busy and distracted					
Knows my ex					
Likes to go to the movies					
Listens to everything I have to say					
Loves to be outdoors					
Lunches with me					
Meditates with me					
Meets me for dinner					
Provides religious/spiritual comfort					
Recommends solutions to problems					
Says it like it is					
Supports me at work					
Tells me the truth					
Understands my break-up issues					
Welcomes calls any time					
Will work out with me					

SECTION I – The Process

CHAPTER **3 – Managing Stress and Thoughts**

Managing Stress and Thoughts

Exercises	Facilitator Tips	Page
Relieving Stress: Breathe ... Breathe ... Breathe	Read the Breathing Exercise aloud. Ask participants to try it as you read it again. Afterwards, ask for reactions. Distribute handouts for participants to take home.	73
Guided Imagery	Read the guided imagery script in a soft, soothing voice. Afterwards, ask participants for their reactions. Ask if they would do this at home when they need to relax.	74
Relaxation Techniques	After you read each relaxation technique, ask for a show of hands of who has done this technique before. If time allows, ask what kind of success with the technique.	75
Present Moment Awareness	Encourage the participants to breathe 2 - 3 deep, relaxing breaths. Read this Present Moment Awareness exercise slowly and calmly. After, allow for a few moments of silence. Then, ask for reactions.	76
Checklist of Enjoyable Activities	Begin the session with this quote by Anne Wilson Schaef: "When we need these healing times, there is nothing better than a good long walk. It is amazing how the rhythmic movements of the feet and legs are so intimately attached to cobweb cleaners in the brain." Ask participants for their reaction to the quotation. After the handout has been completed, ask participants which activity is the one they are most likely to do.	77
Coping with "IF ONLY"	Begin the session with this quote by Myla Kabat-Zinn: "Each difficult moment has the potential to open my eyes and open my heart." Ask participants what the quotation means to them. Distribute handouts and first, read the examples: If only I had listened more. I would have heard what the problem was. If only I had shared more of my feelings. This wouldn't have come as such a surprise to my partner.	78
Journaling	After handouts are completed, ask for a show of hands in response to these questions: *Who already journals? Those of you who do not, what stops you?*	79
I Feel Good	After participants have completed the handout, ask for volunteers to share other items they feel good about that they wrote in the bottom of the page lines.	80
My Regrets	After distributing the handouts, read this example: I shouldn't have made promises I couldn't keep. Rewrite: I am more aware and careful about promises I make now. After the exercise has been completed, ask for volunteers to tell about what they learned from this handout regarding future relationships of any kind.	81
Accentuate the Positive	After handouts are completed, ask what is meant by *It is what it is*.	82
Grateful! Seven Days a Week	Prior to distributing the handout read this quotation by Brian Tracy: "Develop an attitude of gratitude, and give thanks for everything that happens to you, knowing that every step forward is a step toward achieving something bigger and better than your current situation." After participants have completed their handouts, ask for volunteers to share one (or more if time permits) of their own thankfulness.	83
Positive Self-Talk	Example: My Negative Self-Talk: *I should have done better.* My Positive Self-Talk: *I did the best I could at the time.*	84

(Continued on the next page)

SECTION I – The Process

Managing Stress and Thoughts *(Continued)*

Exercises	Facilitator Tips	Page

The Message of the Serenity Prayer	After the handouts are completed, read the following Chinese proverb aloud.
	   "You cannot prevent the birds of sorrow from flying over your head,
	   but you can prevent them from building nests in your hair."
	Ask for reactions and compare it to the Serenity Prayer.
		85

Saying *Hello* to New Dreams	Offer the following example prior to distributing the handouts: *I have always dreamed of going on a major vacation to Peru. My partner didn't want to. I am going to search the internet and call a travel agent to try to find a tour to Peru that includes singles. My friend Mary might want to go, but if not, I will go alone and meet people.*	86
How Can I Take Care of Myself?	*Examples:* Emotional needs *(counselor, therapist, support group)* Physical health *(doctor, dentist, ob/gyn)* Nurture yourself *(warm bath, massage)* Give yourself a break *(Treat myself to lunch at a restaurant)* Know what is under your control, and what isn't *(Breaking up isn't, how I handle it is under my control)* Allow yourself to feel *(laugh, cry)* Keep expectations realistic *(know that the children will be confused, sad)* No hasty decisions *(moving or committing to a new relationship)* Time for fun *(movies, going out)* Take time for yourself *(get a baby sitter, find alone time)* Not a time to start bad habits, even if tempting *(drinking, smoking)* Stay healthy *(hygiene, nutrition, exercise, work-out)* Let anger out in a healthy way *(run, talk about it with trusted person)* Make some changes *(paint a room, hobby, take up a new hobby)* Enjoy *(movies, TV, music)* Know that it is OK to have intense feelings *(sadness, frustration)* Move on by *(dating, vacationing, planning my life)*	87–88
It's OK to Cry	Prior to distributing the handouts, read this quotation by Charles Dickens, and discuss it with the participants: *" We need never be ashamed of our tears."*	89
A MUST - Keeping Your Sense of Humor	After handout is completed, ask participants other ways they can laugh or enjoy life. *(Go to a comedy club, read the funny pages, do something silly, play with a pet, host game night with friends, check out humor books, try karaoke, go to a laughter yoga class.)*	90

Positive Affirmations	Read this anonymous quotation, emphasizing the need for affirmations:
	   "I am my best friend. I need to treat me with dignity and respect, and
	   most importantly, I need to be compassionate with me. I need to accept
	   me in whatever state and condition I am in."
	Suggest that participants cut the affirmations out that resonate with them and tape them in various places at home and work, as reminders.
		91

CHAPTER **3** – **Managing Stress and Thoughts**

Relieving Stress: Breathe...Breathe...Breathe

The mind-body connection is powerful and sometimes ignored.

When we are experiencing a lot of stress, our bodies react as well as our minds. We often aren't even aware of how much tension we carry in our bodies. If we reduce the physical part of stress, we can help reduce our anxiety, worry and distress.

Breathing is the key to relieving the physical part of stress.

Breathing Exercise

Deep, slow, gentle abdominal breaths.
Practice breathing in just this way.
If you wish, you can close your eyes.

As you exhale, imagine that the tension in your body is seeping down from your head, shoulders, belly, thighs, lower legs and down into the floor through your feet.

Notice any parts of your body that still feel stiff. With the next exhale, imagine the breath moving through that part of your body, and flowing down and out through your feet.

As you exhale again, say something soothing and meaningful to yourself (a mantra). For example, "I'm safe," "It's going to be all right," "I'll get through this."

With each exhale, visualize your body becoming more and more relaxed. With each exhale, silently repeat your mantra.

Each day, try inhaling at the count of four and exhaling at the count of six.

**Repeat this breathing throughout the day,
not just when you have a distressing thought or experience.**

SECTION **I – The Process**

Guided Imagery

Guided imagery is a relaxation technique that you can customize for yourself. Here's how it works:

Sit or lie in a comfortable postion with your eyes closed.

Take two or three deep breaths.

Think of a place you've been or imagine one that is peaceful, pleasant and safe.

Picture yourself going to that place.

What do you see as you move forward?

Hear? Smell? Feel on your skin? Perhaps taste?

Notice all the details of where you are.

Keep breathing deeply, feeling yourself transported to this special place.

Keep noticing the details of your place as you continue to move forward.

When you feel ready to come back to the present, slowly open your eyes as you continue to breathe deeply and feel your body relaxing.

You may also find guided imagery CDs helpful.

Relaxation Techniques

Reducing stress and tension is particularly important when you are dealing with the emotional, practical and demanding aspects of ending a committed relationship.

A number of different ways help reduce stress. You may have some ways you've found that are particularly useful for you or some you would like to try. Add any others to the list.

Check list of relaxation techniques	I do this already	I'm willing to try	No thanks!
Bask in the sunlight, even if you're indoors			
Breathe deeply			
Chat with a friend			
Enjoy aromatherapy			
Exercise			
Garden			
Go for a walk outdoors			
Have fun with a pet			
Journal			
Laugh aloud			
Listen to soothing music			
Play with a child			
Practice progressive muscle relaxation			
Relax in a warm bath			
Relieve tension with massage			
Sing, dance, play an instrument, write, etc.			
Stay in the present moment with meditation			
Take a "time out"			
Try Tai Chi or QiGong			
Try Yoga			
Use guided imagery			
Volunteer			
OTHER			
OTHER			
OTHER			
OTHER			

Present Moment Awareness

Anxiety involves regret about the past and worry about the future.

When we are "fully present," we don't feel anxious.

Being in the present can sometimes be difficult when our thoughts are flooding our minds.

When your mind goes to the past or focuses on the future, ask yourself, *"What about right now?"*

To help you to be in the *right now* and quiet those troubling thoughts, use this exercise.

PRESENT MOMENT AWARENESS EXERCISE

- Begin slow easy breathing.

- Visualize the tension in your body seeping down into the floor.

- Look around.

- Begin to name aloud, or to yourself, the things you notice:

    Colors
    Sights
    Shapes
    Sounds
    Smells
    Objects
    Temperature
    Your body relaxing
    How your skin feels

Continue noticing until your mind and body are calmer.

CHAPTER **3 – Managing Stress and Thoughts**

Checklist of Enjoyable Activities

Having an enjoyable time is good! It reduces stress, reminds us that life is more than stress, worry, responsibility, change and loss.

Below is a list of enjoyable activities. Put a check in the box ☑ before those you already enjoy doing. Then put a check ☑ after the ones you'd like to try. Add your own at the end of the list.

- ❑ Be alone ❑
- ❑ Bowl ❑
- ❑ Create a gift for someone special ❑
- ❑ Dance or playing music ❑
- ❑ Decorate a room ❑
- ❑ Do a crossword puzzle ❑
- ❑ Draw ❑
- ❑ Dress up ❑
- ❑ Enjoy a movie ❑
- ❑ Enroll in a class ❑
- ❑ Entertain friends ❑
- ❑ Exercise at the gym ❑
- ❑ Finish a project ❑
- ❑ Give or receive a hug ❑
- ❑ Go on a bike ride ❑
- ❑ Hike ❑
- ❑ Join a volleyball team ❑
- ❑ Knit or participate in another craft ❑
- ❑ Laugh aloud ❑
- ❑ Light scented candles ❑
- ❑ Listen to music or singing ❑
- ❑ Lunch with a friend ❑
- ❑ Nap ❑
- ❑ Paint a picture ❑

- ❑ Plan a vacation ❑
- ❑ Play a game with my children ❑
- ❑ Read a trashy novel ❑
- ❑ Say "no" ❑
- ❑ Select an appealing aroma therapy scent ❑
- ❑ Sip coffee or tea in a shop ❑
- ❑ Sleep in ❑
- ❑ Soak in a tub ❑
- ❑ Star gaze ❑
- ❑ Take part in a book group ❑
- ❑ Tell someone "I love you." ❑
- ❑ Think about my personal accomplishments ❑
- ❑ Try a new sport ❑
- ❑ Walk in the rain ❑
- ❑ Watch a favorite TV program ❑
- ❑ Window shop ❑
- ❑ Write in a journal ❑
- ❑ _____
- ❑ _____
- ❑ _____
- ❑ _____
- ❑ _____
- ❑ _____
- ❑ _____

SECTION I – **The Process**

Coping with "IF ONLY"

> *For all sad words of tongue and pen,
> the saddest are these, 'It might have been.'*
> ~ John Greenleaf Whittier

As we learn to accept what is happening as our relationship is ending, we can torture ourselves with "If only I had," or "If only, I hadn't." We may keep repeating the same things about our partner, too. Reviewing how the relationship became so troubled can be useful, but only when you are able to put the "if's" aside, more and more over time.

Rewrite each of the "if only" statements below as a positive statement about how you would do things differently now.

If only I had listened more. _____

If only I had shared more of my feelings. _____

If only I gave more support and compliments. _____

If only I became upset about just the important things. _____

If only I spent more time with my kids. _____

If only my work wasn't the most important thing in my life. _____

If only I was more loyal to my partner than to other people. _____

If only I learned how to control my temper. _____

If only I recognized I had an alcohol / drug problem. _____

If only I hadn't become involved with someone outside my relationship. _____

If only I were more sensitive to my partner's unhappiness. _____

If only I appreciated what I had. _____

If only I hadn't made a commitment when it didn't feel right. _____

If only I listened more and argued less. _____

If only I understood how difficult our family problems were. _____

Journaling

Journaling or keeping a diary is a wonderful way to . . .

- acknowledge my pain
- express my deepest feelings
- honor my experience
- notice my progress
- notice what's gone well
- vent pent up feelings

Journaling tips:

- Find an attractive journal, or binder for your entries.
- Start now.
- Journal every day. Some people find that making in a journal entry at the same time every day helps them develop the habit.
- Try writing longhand. Since so many of us use the computer, writing out your thoughts, feelings, wishes, etc. makes them more personal and special.
- Just write. Don't be concerned if it makes sense, is important to say, or grammatically correct.
- Don't be concerned about the length of whatever you write.
- Use a pen that feels good in your hand and writes smoothly. Choose different colors.
- Give yourself a goal, like writing something every single day, even if you write, "I can't think of anything to write."
- Don't self-edit. This may be the one place where you can say exactly what you feel and think, without censoring it.
- Use your journal to capture your dreams!

Try writing today's journal entry now. You may want to write about what is most important at the moment, what you're looking forward to, what concerns you, what you accomplished, what you are feeling, etc.

Today's journaling date: _____

_____
_____
_____
_____
_____
_____
_____

Some people like to express themselves through the arts, drawing, dancing, listening or playing music, poetry, etc., as well as journaling.

SECTION I – **The Process**

My Regrets

Second guessing serves no purpose unless it helps us learn and try to do better in the future. We all have regrets. In the midst of a situation, like the end of a committed relationship, we may have many regrets about things we did, and about things we didn't do but now wish we had. Changing our thinking from our regrets to what might be done in the future might ease the regrets.

These sentences express regret. Rewrite the sentences that apply to you in order for them to be less blaming, more kind and accepting. And remember, everyone does and says things at some point that they regret. (Continue writing on the back.)

- I shouldn't have made promises I couldn't keep.
  _____

- I wish I had said "I love you" more.
  _____

- I criticized too much.
  _____

- I tried to change my partner.
  _____

- I didn't stay true to my vows.
  _____

- I should have admitted I was wrong.
  _____

- I should have accepted some of the blame more often.
  _____

- I could have given more compliments.
  _____

- I wish I hadn't given up my career.
  _____

- I should have paid more attention to finances.
  _____

- I shouldn't have dropped out of school.
  _____

- I wish I had left sooner.
  _____

- I regret making it all about me.
  _____

- I regret making it all about the kids.
  _____

- I wish I had been more true to myself.
  _____

- I could have accepted my partner for who he/she was.
  _____

- I feel badly about how I ended the relationship.
  _____

- I could have been more direct about what I wanted and needed.
  _____

CHAPTER 3 – Managing Stress and Thoughts

I Feel Good

No matter how long a committed relationship lasts, at times a break up might be inevitable. Look back and give yourself a pat on the back for the things that you feel good about yourself during and with the ending of this relationship. Check each box that pertains to you and add other thoughts in the lines at the bottom of the page.

- ❑ I grew into a better person.
- ❑ I admitted I was wrong.
- ❑ I continued my education.
- ❑ I had some fun times.
- ❑ I had some good years.
- ❑ I have a career.
- ❑ I have become stronger.
- ❑ I have built a network of close supportive friends.
- ❑ I have child(ren).
- ❑ I have forgiven my partner (not necessarily forgotten).
- ❑ I have forgiven myself.
- ❑ I have learned that I have family members I can depend on.
- ❑ I now accept the break up.
- ❑ I have learned what and who I want in my life.
- ❑ I have made healthy decisions for my children.
- ❑ I have made healthy decisions for myself.
- ❑ I kept my promises and my vows.
- ❑ I learned to be assertive.
- ❑ I left before it became uglier.
- ❑ I realize I am not solely to blame and that it takes two people to make a marriage work.
- ❑ I tried to make the relationship work.
- ❑ I was direct about my needs and wants.
- ❑ I was honest about my feelings.
- ❑ I was true to myself.
- ❑ I know, no matter what, I will survive.
- ❑ _____
- ❑ _____
- ❑ _____

SECTION I – **The Process**

Accentuate the Positive

Staying positive during a breakup isn't easy, especially if one or both spouses are angry or resentful. This creates more pain and prevents or delays healing from taking place. Several ways can make it easier.

Check those below that apply to you and write your own on the blanks.

- ❏ Accept that *it is what it is!*
- ❏ Accept that your partner came from a different background from yours.
- ❏ Accept that your partner did the best he/she could, given his/her relationship skills.
- ❏ Acknowledge your feelings as they arise.
- ❏ Be aware that your children will benefit if you and your partner get along.
- ❏ Cry away negative feelings.
- ❏ Exercise.
- ❏ Focus on the good that you received from the relationship.
- ❏ Forgive your partner.
- ❏ Forgive yourself.
- ❏ Know that you did the best you could.
- ❏ Lift your head up high and move on.
- ❏ Process and be aware of your emotions so they will not be silenced.
- ❏ Release the resentment or anger you have been holding on to.
- ❏ Smile and laugh.
- ❏ Socialize.
- ❏ Surround yourself with patient and caring family and friends.
- ❏ _____
- ❏ _____
- ❏ _____
- ❏ _____
- ❏ _____
- ❏ _____

Grateful! Seven Days a Week

Seven things for which we can be grateful:

See
Hear
Touch
Taste
Feel
Laugh
Love

What are seven other things for which you are grateful? Explain why.

1) _____
   _____

2) _____
   _____

3) _____
   _____

4) _____
   _____

5) _____
   _____

6) _____
   _____

7) _____
   _____

SECTION I – The Process

Positive Self-Talk

Self-Talk refers to internal monologues that can have a positive or negative influence. Reframe the negative self-talk below to positive self-talk.

My Negative Self-Talk	My Positive Self-Talk
I should have done better.	
I will never recover from losing my partner.	
I hate when I cry. It shows that I am weak.	
I'll never date again!	
My confidence is gone.	
The children will never forgive me.	

Often we talk in a more polite and understanding, compassionate way to other people that we talk to ourselves. Now, list YOUR negative self-talk and reframe each one in a positive way.

My Negative Self-Talk	My Positive Self-Talk

The Message of the Serenity Prayer

Most of us are familiar with the Serenity Prayer:

Grant me the serenity to accept the things I cannot change,
courage to change the things I can and wisdom to know the difference.

When a committed relationship is ending, our lives may seem to be completely out of control. So, we try very hard to control just about everything and become frustrated and more anxious as a result.

State your challenges and use the Serenity Prayer to work out the control issue. Think about the challenges you are facing. Which can you change and which must you accept.

My Challenge	Can I Change It? Yes or No?	What I CAN do about It

SECTION I – The Process

Saying *Hello* to New Dreams

Important losses we experience when a committed relationship ends are the dreams we had for our life together.

As we create a new life for ourselves, it is time to allow ourselves to dream again, and see the possibility of realizing new dreams or reconstructing the dreams of the past. We need to realize that life can hold both positive and negative experiences and it's up to us to be open to the possibilities of the positives in our future.

Some of our fondest dreams may still come true by making careful choices that lead to positive outcomes. Making room for new dreams might mean recreating or adapting the old ones.

Write about a dream you once had that you now realize won't happen in the way you imagined.

_____
_____
_____
_____
_____
_____

Now, rewrite the dream in a way that seems attainable for you.

_____
_____
_____
_____
_____
_____
_____
_____
_____
_____
_____
_____
_____
_____

CHAPTER 3 – **Managing Stress and Thoughts**

How Can I Take Care of Myself?

Going through a breakup takes its toll. It can be a time of loss of companionship, shared experiences, financial, intellectual, social and emotional support, and hopes, plans and dreams. It is now a time for you to take care of you! Note ways you can take care of yourself.

Meet my emotional needs _____
_____
_____
_____

Build and maintain my physical health _____
_____
_____

Nurture myself _____
_____
_____
_____
_____

Give myself a break _____
_____
_____
_____
_____

Acknowledge what is under my control, and what isn't_____
_____
_____
_____

Allow myself to feel _____
_____
_____
_____

Keep my expectations realistic _____
_____
_____
_____

Avoid hasty decisions _____
_____
_____
_____

(Continued on the next page)

How I Can Take Care of Myself (Continued)

Find time for fun _____
_____
_____
_____

Take time for myself _____
_____
_____
_____

Avoid starting bad habits now, even if they are tempting _____
_____
_____
_____

Find healthy ways to release anger _____
_____
_____
_____

Make some changes _____
_____
_____
_____

Enjoy nature _____
_____
_____
_____

Know that it is OK to have intense feelings _____
_____
_____
_____

Move on by _____
_____
_____
_____

Find relaxation techniques that will work for me _____
_____
_____
_____

CHAPTER 3 – **Managing Stress and Thoughts**

It's OK to Cry!

Often, we feel better after crying and feel ready to tackle the world, one step at a time. However it is sometimes difficult to cry.

**What stops us from crying? Are any of these true for you?
If you have other reasons, write them on the blank lines at the end of the list.**

- ❑ People tell me to stay strong (for myself, the children and/or others).
- ❑ I feel I need to stay strong (for myself, the children and/or others).
- ❑ I don't want to burden anyone with my pain.
- ❑ I'm concerned people won't want to be with me.
- ❑ I believe people think I should be over it by now.
- ❑ I'm afraid if I will start crying I will never be able to stop.
- ❑ I remember being told, Stop that crying or I'll give you a reason to cry.
- ❑ I refuse to admit I'm hurting.
- ❑ _____
- ❑ _____
- ❑ _____

**If you have difficulty crying, look at these tips on how to get those tears flowing.
Write any tips that you have.**

- Watch a tear-jerking movie or television show.
- Look at old photographs.
- Cut an onion!
- Use typical body movements and sounds of crying.
- Listen to a song that rekindles memories.
- _____
- _____
- _____
- _____

SECTION I – **The Process**

A MUST – Keeping your Sense of Humor

Laughter is powerful and a wonderful way to defuse conflict. When laughter is shared, it brings people together. When we can laugh at ourselves or our situation, it keeps us grounded. A good laugh adds joy to the moment, eases tension, relieves stress and can put us in a better frame of mind.

When did you last laugh with someone? How did it feel?
_____
_____

What tickles your funny bone, time and time again? _____
_____

Write about a time you had an uncontrollable, huge belly laugh _____
_____

What movies or television shows appeal to your sense of humor. Have you watched them lately? ____
_____

What is your favorite memory of laughter with your family? _____
_____

What is your favorite memory of laughter with your ex? _____
_____

Name a time when you made someone else laugh when they needed a good laugh. How did you feel?
_____

Tell about a time you were able to laugh at yourself and/or your imperfections? _____
_____
_____

Can you remember a specific joke that makes you laugh when you think about it? _____
_____
_____

Do you have a memory that makes you laugh every time you think of it? _____
_____

**Laughter can lift our spirits and not just in the moment.
That good feeling can stay on and on.**
Try it!

CHAPTER **3 – Managing Stress and Thoughts**

Positive Affirmations

Affirmations are healing, positive statements you say to yourself.

I believe in myself.	I inspire others with my actions.	I embrace change.
Good things are coming my way.	I am hopeful.	I deserve to lead a wonderful and prosperous life.
I am flexible.	*I face every day with a kind spirit.*	I am a survivor!
I gain emotional strength each day.	I feel safe within myself.	My body feels healthy and at ease.
I am confident I can handle any challenge.	I don't have to figure it all out now.	**I focus on the positive.**
WRITE YOUR OWN AFFIRMATION	WRITE YOUR OWN AFFIRMATION	WRITE YOUR OWN AFFIRMATION

Helping the Children through the Breakup

Exercises	Facilitator Tips	Page
What the Children May Ask	After handouts are completed, ask participants if there were any questions that were very difficult to answer. Ask them to brainstorm possible responses and write them on the back of the handout. Suggest to participants that they share their responses to the questions with their partners to allow them to both be on the same page.	95
Co-Parenting Basics	After distributing the handouts, encourage participants to think about the positive and negative aspects of the co-parenting agreement and to add other statements of concern.	96
Parenting Issues after a Breakup	After handouts have been completed, ask participants what they envision for the next holiday.	97
What to Say?	Ask participants to come up with any other sentences to complete. Then discuss the importance of collaborating with their partners about what to say in order to be consistent and avoid confusion.	98
Where Will I Live?	After the handout has been completed, ask participants to brainstorm other questions their children might ask and how they can respond.	99
I'm Most Worried About	Use this exercise as an opportunity to brainstorm, thus reassuring participants that their worries can be addressed. After completing the handouts, ask each participant to share one of the checked worries and request other group members to offer suggestions of how to alleviate the worry.	100
We Agree about the Children	Prior to participants working on the handout, ask them to limit negative comments and place emphasis on both parents wanting what's best for their children.	101–102
My Goals as a Parent	After the handouts have been completed, discuss each item separately and brainstorm how the goals can be reached.	103
I Expect My Child to …	Encourage participants to recognize each child as an individual and complete a separate handout for each child. After they have completed the handout, ask for volunteers to share their responses to the last question, *What I want most for my child is* _____.	104
Red Flags	Distribute to participants one handout for each child, no matter what the child's age. Emphasize and discuss the last paragraph on the page.	105
Different Strokes	After participants have completed the handout, ask which situations will be problems.	106

Impact of a Breakup on Adult Children	Ask participants: What role does your adult child have? These roles are usually established well before the marriage ends.
	    The problem-solver who might feel responsible for fixing the marriage.
	    The neutral negotiator (mediator) who is more objective than the problem-solver.
	    The first among equals – the leader of the siblings. The "it's not my problem, don't bother me" child.
		107

SECTION I – **The Process**

Helping the Children through the Breakup
(Continued)

Exercises	Facilitator Tips	Page
What Will the Children Think if I Date?	After handouts have been completed, ask participants to share other issues their children may worry about.	108
Dating When Children are Involved	After participants have completed the handout, ask for volunteers to share responses to the last question.	109
The Twelve Commandments of Co-Parenting	Ask twelve volunteers to each read a commandment. Discuss how they can follow these commandments.	110

What the Children May Ask

Talking to your children about breaking up may be one of the most difficult parts of the process. They might be surprised, relieved, scared, angry and/or embarrassed. Their feelings may change from day to day, even from minute to minute. Their reactions when you tell them depend to a fair degree on their ages and, of course, their personalities, as well as what you say and how you say it. Experts agree that ideally, you and your partner should tell the children together and deliver the same message. Then be ready for the questions and emotions your announcement will provoke.

Here are some questions your children might ask.
Be prepared by thinking ahead and writing your answers below.

- Where will I live? _____

- Who will take care of me? _____

- Are you doing this because I was bad? _____

- Don't you love each other anymore? _____

- What about my toys? _____

- Will I have to change schools? _____

- Why are you doing this to me? _____

- Whose idea was this? _____

- Can I tell my friends? How do I do it? _____

- Why can't you get along? _____

- What took you so long? _____

SECTION I – **The Process**

Co-Parenting Basics

When children are involved, a co-parenting agreement is part of the final decree issued by the court before a divorce becomes final.

Finish these sentence starters as you think about putting your co-parenting agreement into action.

- I feel confident that we will be able to live by the co-parenting agreement because _____

- I am particularly satisfied with the agreement because _____

- One aspect of the co-parenting agreement that I am worried about is _____

- As we co-parent, we need to pay special attention to _____

- We need to make sure the children understand _____
  _____ as stated in the agreement.

- With regard to this agreement, family members need to _____

- Initially, I think it's important to _____

- A third party could help us negotiate and cooperate as co-parents _____

- _____

CHAPTER 4 – **Helping the Children through the Breakup**

Parenting Issues after a Breakup

After a breakup, parents deal with many issues.

Check the ones you believe might be your issues:

- ❑ Decent, amicable relationship with the partner
  We can make plans and arrangements and stay united for the sake of the children.
- ❑ Custody and time-sharing
  Where children stay, how they go from one place to the other, who else can pick up the children, etc.
- ❑ Contact with children when they are with the other parent
  Cooperation with the partner: share cell phone, email, phone schedules.
- ❑ Family birthdays.
  Where and when? One party or two?
- ❑ Holidays
  Alternating holidays each year, splitting the day, certain holidays for each person, sharing time during long vacations.
- ❑ Different religious and spiritual views
  Which to practice, where to attend and how often..
- ❑ School
  Which school, college planning, etc.
- ❑ Activities – After school and weekends
  Decisions to cover which after school and weekend activities, lessons, sports, music, etc.
- ❑ Old enough?
  Dating ground rules, house rules, cell phone, driving, owning a car, etc.
- ❑ Agreements and guidelines
  TV time and shows, choice of movies, junk food, driving with other friends, punishments.
- ❑ Health
  Under whose insurance, making school and medical appointments, notifying the other person with a health issue and/or emergency, decisions about physical and mental health issues, etc.
- ❑ Extras
  School vacations, uninsured medical expenses, extracurricular activities, cell phone, etc.

List some other issues that you feel you may encounter.

_____

_____

_____

> **Remember to inform the children's teachers and counselors about the situation. Continue to provide updates.**

SECTION I – **The Process**

What to Say?

The biggest source of problems for children when their parents split up is being put in the middle, or having to choose one parent or the other.

Deciding what to say to the children when you're breaking up is difficult, especially if only one of you has made the decision, while the other is resisting or upset at the idea. It is best if you and your partner can agree to what you think will be the *most helpful for your children* at this time of crisis in the family.

Complete the sentence starters as you formulate what you might say.

We've decided to _____

_____

We've made this decision because _____

_____

We think that this will be_____

_____

We want you to know _____

_____

This doesn't mean _____

_____

Remember that_____

_____

Add any other thoughts that you might want to bring into the conversation._____

_____

_____

_____

_____

_____

_____

CHAPTER 4 – **Helping the Children through the Breakup**

Where Will I Live?

Once one or both of you has made the decision to separate, careful planning will make the change as easy as possible for the children. Rushing to have one of you out of the house is ill-advised. You will be faced with your children's inevitable questions.

Below are some questions your children will probably ask.
Use this page to *rehearse* your responses:

Do I have to move? _____
_____

Who is going to move? Where? _____
_____

When? _____
_____

Will there be room for me? _____
_____

When will I be with you? (or your partner) _____
_____

When will I talk to you? (or your partner) _____
_____

Will I have my things there? _____
_____

Will I see me grandma and grandpa? My aunts and uncles and cousins?_____
_____

How will I see my friends? _____
_____

Will I go to the same school? _____
_____

What and when should I tell my friends?_____
_____

SECTION I – **The Process**

I'm Most Worried About

When you and your family go through this traumatic change of a relationship ending, you will experience many worries that go along with the new reality in your life. By identifying the concerns and coming up with ways of handling them, you can help yourself and your family move forward.

Check the concerns you've been worrying about. Write how you might address these issues.

❑ Dealing with my children's reactions and behavior _____
_____

❑ Losing my extended family _____

❑ Continuing (physically and financially) my children's extracurricular activities _____

❑ Maintaining consistent discipline of the children _____

❑ Spending enough time with the children _____

❑ Fixing repairs _____

❑ Finishing household repairs _____

❑ Finding time for myself _____

❑ Feeling isolated _____

❑ Caring for the children alone _____

❑ Dealing with children's emergencies and everyday traumas alone _____

❑ Maintaining family traditions _____

❑ Losing friends who have taken sides _____

OTHER WORRIES
_____
_____
_____

CHAPTER 4 – **Helping the Children through the Breakup**

We Agree about the Children . . .

When a committed relationship is ending, people most often think about the ways they disagree. It is important to remember what you DO agree about, especially when it comes to the children.

Note ways both you and your partner *agree* on the issues listed below. If you and your partner cannot yet agree on an issue, leave the lines blank.

Family _____
_____

Curfews _____
_____

Respect for adults _____
_____

Respect for other people's things_____
_____

Kind treatment of others_____
_____

Homework and grades in school _____
_____

Schoolwork rewards or negative consequences _____
_____

Allowances_____
_____

Religious observance _____
_____

(Continued on the next page)

SECTION I – **The Process**

We Agree about the Children *(Continued)*

Time allotted for TV, computer, phone, video games and other electronic equipment _____
_____

Social networking _____
_____

Fashionable clothes and fads _____
_____

Sports _____
_____

Travel _____
_____

Chores _____
_____

Discipline _____
_____

Extra curricular activities _____
_____

Other: _____
_____
_____
_____

CHAPTER **4** – Helping the Children through the Breakup

My Goals as a Parent

Parenting with a partner is definitely different from being a single parent. As a single parent, you can feel overwhelmed. However, reshaping your day-to-day life can give you a greater sense of control and help you be proactive as you move forward.

Start with thinking about what you want for yourself and your children once you are no longer living with the children's other parent. In the box before the statement check ☑ the items that are most important to you. For the items you think you can begin to work on in the next month, put a check in the box ☑ at the end of the statement.

- ❏ Spend quality time with each child. ❏
- ❏ Tuck each child into bed every night the child is with you. ❏
- ❏ Share a small positive conversation each night with older children. ❏
- ❏ Read a story to each young child every night. ❏
- ❏ Arrange play dates with children's friends. ❏
- ❏ Join a group in which you and the children can do things together. ❏
- ❏ Talk directly to your ex instead of asking the children to carry messages. ❏
- ❏ Honor the terms of the co-parenting agreement. ❏
- ❏ Accept and support each child's feelings regardless of what those feelings are. ❏
- ❏ Make time to take care of yourself so you can take care of them. ❏
- ❏ Help them understand the ways in which life has stayed the same as well as changed. ❏
- ❏ Find other adults to talk to rather than expecting a child to be a substitute parent or partner. ❏
- ❏ Establish and discuss with children a household routine that remains stable for everyone. ❏
- ❏ Get professional advice if your children's behavior, habits and overall functioning seem to be deteriorating over time. ❏
- ❏ Apologize to children if and when you lose your temper. ❏
- ❏ Empathize with each child's distress. ❏
- ❏ Talk openly about the children's experiences of loss and change. ❏
- ❏ _____
- ❏ _____
- ❏ _____
- ❏ _____
- ❏ _____
- ❏ _____

SECTION I – **The Process**

I Expect My Child to...

Your child's reaction to the new realities of your family's life may be expected or, on the other hand, may surprise you. Use a separate page for each child and complete the sentences.

Child's Name _____

I expect my child to react to the breakup by _____

To feel safe, my child needs _____

My child needs help _____

My child is most concerned when _____

My child shows personal feelings _____

My child is very emotional about _____

For this child, school _____

My child's greatest strength is _____

My child will probably blame _____ for the breakup because _____

My child will be sure the breakup _____

I'm confident my child will _____

What I want most for my child is _____

CHAPTER 4 – Helping the Children through the Breakup

Red Flags

Children's adjustments to their parents' breakup often depends on the level of conflict between the parents. While we expect our children to have their ups and downs – particularly when their whole life seems to be changing without their permission – we need to pay attention to warning signs that can suggest that a professional evaluation is merited.

Normal reactions to separation

Anger . . . . Children may express their anger, rage, and resentment with you and your partner for taking away what they're used to.

Anxiety . . . . Children are likely to feel anxious when dealing with such a huge change in the family.

Sadness . . . . Children will feel the change which is a loss to everyone in the family.

Mild Depression . . . When feeling sad is combined with feelings of helplessness and hopelessness, children may show signs of depression.

Working through these feelings about the breakup is likely to take some time, but gradually you should see an improvement, perhaps with some set-backs, along the way. If anxiety, sadness and other distress signals seem to be getting worse after a short while, and are accompanied by some of the following signs, seek professional advice. Complete one handout for each child.

Check the reactions you are noticing of _____ after the breakup.
NAME OF CHILD

- ❑ Anxiety about rejection
- ❑ Change in friendships
- ❑ Concerns expressed by professionals such as teachers
- ❑ Constant irritability
- ❑ Continuous feelings of hopelessness and worthlessness
- ❑ Drug or alcohol abuse
- ❑ Excessive crying
- ❑ Frequent angry or violent outbursts
- ❑ Inability to function in normal activities
- ❑ Increase or decrease in appetite
- ❑ Poor concentration
- ❑ Refusal to pursue activities formerly enjoyed
- ❑ School problems
- ❑ Self-injury, cutting or eating disorders
- ❑ Sleep issues
- ❑ Social withdrawal
- ❑ Talk of suicide
- ❑ Withdrawal from social activities and loved ones

If the anxiety, sadness and other distresses seem to be getting worse after some months, and are accompanied by some of the above signals, seek professional advice. If the child expresses thoughts of suicide or dying – seek professional help immediately.

SECTION I – **The Process**

Different Strokes

You and your co-parent are likely to have some differences in setting and maintaining the rules for your children. It is all right to have different rules, but the rules in each household need to be as explicit as possible so the children know what to expect and what is expected of them. The key is consistency, even if it is a different consistency in each home. The key also is not to be in competition – Who is nicest? Who lets the children get away with more?

Talk to your co-parent about the rules for each household, *not to argue about them*, but to clarify the expectations in each place. Then write down what you each expect so everyone will know how things will work in each place. If what you write below needs to be changed at any point, make revisions together, and give the co-parent a copy.

No matter what they are, your house rules should include a reward-and-consequence system that applies to everyone. For example, if one of your rules is that nobody eats in the living room, then nobody eats in the living room, parents included. You can't build a strong family team in a "Do as I say, not as I do" environment.

Situation	Your Rules	The Co-Parent's Rules
Allowance and/or extra money		
Bedtime		
Behavior		
Chores		
Complaining about other parent		
Computer (and other electronic equipment) hours		
Curfew		
Homework time		
Household chores		
Laundry		
Play time		
Punishments, time-outs and other consequences		
Respectful talk		
Telephone, email or texting time		
Television hours		
Where and what to eat		
Other		
Other		

Impact of a Breakup on Adult Children

For adult children, a parental breakup can be just as traumatic as it is for young children. Check the boxes that apply to your situation with your adult child.
Use a separate sheet for each child.

Adult Child's Name _____

Which of these issues will have an impact on your adult child in the case of a breakup?
- ❏ The need to, for one or both of the parents, to receive excessive emotional support.
- ❏ One or both parents wanting the adult child to take sides.
- ❏ Unrealistic expectations of one or both of the parents.
- ❏ Pressure on the adult child to return to live with the abandoned parent.
- ❏ Expectations of adult child for financial support by one or both parents.
- ❏ The adult child is financially dependent on parents.
- ❏ The adult child is presently living with the parents.

What will your adult children lose when the marriage ends?
- ❏ The family as they knew it.
- ❏ Faith in marriage as an institution.
- ❏ How the breakup will impact on child's future ability to trust and have healthy, intimate relationships.
- ❏ Home as adult child remembers it.
- ❏ Shared family rituals and traditions.
- ❏ Ideals about parents and their marriage.
- ❏ Life as it was.

How will you avoid putting your child in the middle?
- ❏ Do not ask your child to be the message carrier.
- ❏ Do not ask for confidentiality that your child doesn't or can't honor.
- ❏ Don't expect or pressure your child to take your side.
- ❏ Don't recruit your child to support your side in negotiations.
- ❏ Don't bribe or use money, or threat of withholding money, as emotional blackmail.
- ❏ Don't use your child as a confidant.

Which of the following possibilities after the breakup concern you?
- ❏ Disabled or frail parents are less likely to get personal and financial support from children.
- ❏ The parent whose ties to this child are less close is especially vulnerable.
- ❏ Remarriage of one or both parents can put further strain on the parent/child relationship.
- ❏ Remarried parents might receive less financial and emotional support from their children.

You do not need your child's permission to end the relationship. However, it is reasonable for your child to expect to have continuing relationships with both parents, navigate the loyalty bind, set limits, articulate the desire to be left out of the fighting and expect parents to be civil in the child's presence.

SECTION I – **The Process**

What Will the Children Think if I Date?

When you feel ready to date after a breakup, while you don't need your children's permission, you may want to think about how they might react.

How you explain your social life depends in part on the age of your child:
- For preschool age children, you could say that you're going to meet a friend and set a time for when you'll be back.
- For school-age children, you might say that you're going to meet a friend. *"Just like you have special friends, I do, too."*
- For pre and early teens, you might want to ask them how they would feel if you started to date. You're not asking permission, rather providing a way for your children to share feelings about your dating.
- With older children, talking about dating in a more general way may be useful as long as you remember that you're the adult, not two friends chatting about dating.

Your children may worry that ...
- your dating means you and their other parent won't be getting back together.
- they will need to share you with someone else.
- liking the person you're dating is disloyal to the other parent.
- they will have another adult telling them what to do and when to do it.

Other things you feel your child might worry about:

Child's name _____
- _____
- _____
- _____

Child's name _____
- _____
- _____
- _____

Child's name _____
- _____
- _____
- _____

Dating When Children are Involved

The idea of returning to the dating scene after years of being in a serious, committed relationship may be appealing, yet scary! Chances are that sooner or later you will consider dating. Depending on the ages of your children, different issues arise.

How will you know when you are ready to date? _____
_____
_____

To what degree are your children prepared for you to date? _____
_____
_____

Do they wish that you and your partner might get together again? _____
_____
_____

If so, how do you respond to them? _____
_____
_____

How honest have you been with them? _____
_____
_____

What do you say when they express the wish that you'll reunite? _____
_____
_____

You possibly won't want to bring someone you're seeing to meet your children, only to disappoint them if it doesn't work out. How can you manage that? _____
_____
_____

Your partner may also give you a difficult time about your dating. How can you handle that? And now your partner is dating. How will you react? _____
_____
_____

SECTION I – The Process

The Twelve Commandments of Co-Parenting

While your relationship as partners may be at an end, you will always have a relationship with each other as parents.

Take a look at *The Twelve Commandments of Co-Parenting* below.
Can you discuss them with your ex and try to stick by them yourself? If not, why not?

The Twelve Commandments of Co-Parenting

1. Thou shalt talk openly with your child about issues the child raises.

2. Thou shalt not put your child in the middle of your disagreements.

3. Thou shalt honor your child's right to personal feelings.

4. Thou shalt apologize to your child when making a mistake or losing your temper.

5. Thou shalt expect your child to be responsible only for age-appropriate chores.

6. Thou shalt not rely on your child to be the other adult in the household.

7. Thou shalt get professional help if needed for yourself and if indicated for your children.

8. Thou shalt support your child's relationship with your ex's family.

9. Thou shalt approach introducing a new person in your life with sensitivity to the feelings of your child.

10. Thou shalt avoid speaking unkindly of your ex to your child.

11. Thou shalt make a good faith effort to honor your ex as your child's parent.

12. Thou shalt not use your children as a pawn between you and your child's other parent.

CHAPTER 5 – Emerging from Divorce

Emerging from Divorce

Exercises	Facilitator Tips	Page
Who Am I? **Who Am I? I'm_____.**	After handouts are completed, ask participants to share their response to the last question: Who are you?	113
My Hopes and Strengths	Distribute handouts and encourage participants to be candid about the positives. Remind them it's not bragging!	114
New Opportunities	Prior to distributing handout, read the following quote by Nena O'Neill: *"Out of every crisis comes the chance to be reborn; to choose the kind of change that will help us to grow and fulfill ourselves more completely."* After participants complete the handout, ask for a vote on which question they would like to hear others' responses.	115
I'm in Charge of Me	Use this list as a starting place for a homework assignment for more ideas to share the next time.	116
Just for Me	After participants have completed the handouts, ask for volunteers to state which of the items they tend to neglect and why.	117
Routines	Encourage the participants to see this as a draft to be discussed with the children, if they are old enough, at a family meeting. Suggest that perhaps the other parent be involved as well to keep life for the children as consistent as possible.	118
Accepting the Past	After participants complete the handout, ask them what they have accepted from the past. Then ask what they have NOT been able to accept from the past.	119
Letting Go Pointers	Ask participants to pass the paper around the room, each reading one bullet point. After going through the list, ask them to do it again, and invite people to comment and brainstorm on each of the various points.	120
My New Life	Encourage participants to recognize each child as an individual and complete a separate handout for each child. After they have completed the handout, ask for volunteers to share their responses to the last question, *What I want most for my child is _____.*	121
Single Again	After completing the handouts, discuss with participants how priorities were determined. Revisit this exercise from time to time, to adjust over time and to celebrate successes.	122
In the Next Six Months	Ask for volunteers to share one of their goals. After each one, ask if this goal meets the criteria on the handout.	123
Recovery	In the last section of the handouts, if needed, here are a few examples: *Won't cry so often; Will not be so sad every time I see my ex.; Will be able to talk with my ex without feeling angry.*	124
A Different Family but Still Family	Ask participants to share their responses and discuss each situation together as a group. Ask if they would be willing to share their thoughts on the definition of a real family.	125
Coping with Now	Ask participants to share other items to add to the *Coping with Now* list. Then read each item separately and ask them for a show of hands if they think they will be able to do it. If they feel they cannot, ask if they will share why not. Perhaps other participants can give suggestions on how these items can be accomplished.	126

© 2013 WHOLE PERSON ASSOCIATES, 210 WEST MICHIGAN ST., DULUTH MN 55802-1908 ▪ 800-247-6789

SECTION I – **The Process**

Emerging from Divorce (Continued)

Exercises	Facilitator Tips	Page

Old and New Traditions	Possible example:
	    Event *(Birthdays)*
	    Old Traditions *(We always sang Happy Birthday at dinner with cake and ice cream.)*
	    New or Modified Traditions *(We now celebrate at breakfast on the weekend and my ex celebrates at dinner.)*
		127

It's Been a Long Time Since I've Looked for a Job	Encourage participants to develop a group plan to support each others' efforts, share ideas and celebrate steps taken. Examples of community resources are: libraries, community colleges, employment services through non-profit agencies, networking, etc.	128
My Own Dreams	After handouts are completed, suggest that participants ask why not and how, rather than believing that no part of the dream is, or ever will be, possible.	129

Rebuild My Social Life	Distribute handouts and ask what comes to mind with each bulleted guideline. Position each as an experiment to try until it's a good fix.
	Examples of other good ideas are:
	    Start a card game at your home.
	    Invite one person of a couple out for breakfast or lunch.
	    Sign up for a class and arrive early to chat.
	    Revive friendships you let go of in the past.
	    Help people – good for you, for them and for networking.
		130

Community Resources	Examples:
	    Community – *Alumni Association*
	        Advantages – *Reminisce about the past.*
	        Disadvantages – *Many might be happily married.*
	    Community – *Book club.*
	        Advantages – *I'll need to read and be distracted.*
	        Disadvantages – *I may feel stressed to finish a book in time.*
		131

Dating and the Internet	After participants have completed the handouts, ask for volunteers to share other issues they might have about internet dating. Then ask them to share sites they recommend or those they would not recommend.	132

Who Am I? Who Am I? I'm _____

When in a committed relationship, it is natural to compromise with your partner, advocate for your children and spend a lot of your non-working time keeping everyone happy. Especially if you were in a long relationship, you may have given up many things you enjoyed as a single person because they didn't fit with your partner's or family's life. Maybe you loved to go out, but your partner loved staying in. Maybe you loved the theater and your partner loved sports.

You now have the opportunity and choice to create a new life, with new activities, friends and direction. Although you may no longer be one half of a couple, you are 100% of YOU! When there is a break-up, it is time to think about who you are.

What would you like to do with your free time? _____

What activity or adventure will make you excited to get out of bed in the morning? _____

How can you choose to live your life with good feelings? _____

Who is in your support network that will energize you? _____

What did you give up in favor of your relationship? _____

What do you like about yourself? _____

What were your hobbies and activities before the partnership? _____

What is a new side of yourself that you would like to discover? _____

What do you have control over? _____

What is your life purpose at this point in your life? _____

What are your passions? What can you do to indulge in them? _____

Who are you? _____

SECTION I – **The Process**

My Hopes and Strengths

We are shaped in part by our committed relationship. In many ways, our identity rests on the nature of that committed relationship. When it ends, we need to figure out who we are. While that can be somewhat frightening, we also have an opportunity to see ourselves in a new way, and make choices that weren't available to you before.

Respond to the following questions recognizing your strengths and hopes for yourself:

What three words would you use to describe yourself right now?

1)_____ 2) _____ 3) _____

What three words would you like others to use to describe you?

1)_____ 2) _____ 3) _____

What three things in your life are most important to you?

1)_____ 2) _____ 3) _____

What brings you joy? _____
_____

What talents would you like to explore and build on? _____
_____

What are your most positive qualities?_____
_____

Why do you feel people are drawn to you?_____
_____

What aspect of yourself in your relationship would you like to leave behind?_____
_____

What dream have you put aside because of other commitments? _____
_____

Who are you now?_____
_____

CHAPTER 5 – Emerging from Divorce

New Opportunities

As we are adjusting to the loss of a committed relationship, we may begin to think about the things we wish we had done differently. It is an important part of learning from this experience. However, if we dwell on the ways we wish we had done things differently, we may not give ourselves room to be open to new opportunities with which to experiment.

Complete the sentences below about things you would like to do.

1. I would like to say "no" to _____
   _____ less guilt and worry.

2. I would like to try something that I've never done, like_____
   _____ , just for fun.

3. I would like to change _____
   _____about the way I look and dress.

4. I would like to go on _____
   _____ retreat.

5. I would like to become an advocate and/or volunteer for_____
   _____ which is a cause I really believe in.

6. I would like to _____
   _____ which is something that I've always wanted to do.

7. I would to do something silly, like _____
   _____.

8. I would like to _____
   _____ all by myself.

9. I would like to reconnect with _____
   _____ with whom I have lost contact.

10. I would like to explore these job opportunities: _____
    _____.

11. I would like to invite _____
    _____ out for lunch even though I don't know this person well.

12. I would like to _____
    _____.

SECTION I – **The Process**

I'm in Charge of ME

When your committed relationship has ended, you are facing a future for which you probably haven't planned. This is during a time of mixed and powerful emotions that can leave you feeling out of control and helpless. Structuring a plan can help you feel more in charge of your future. In each category below, check at least three items you can do that will ensure a better future. Add others at the end of each category.

YOUR PHYSICAL WELL-BEING
- ❏ Avoid too much alcohol.
- ❏ Reduce the caffeine and sugar you consume.
- ❏ Stop smoking if you do now.
- ❏ Exercise regularly.
- ❏ Take up meditation.
- ❏ Eat nutritious meals.
- ❏ Drink plenty of water.
- ❏ Get to bed at a consistent time and get enough sleep for your particular body.
- ❏ _____

EMOTIONAL WELL-BEING
- ❏ Do something special for yourself every day, regardless of how small it might seem.
- ❏ Before you go to sleep every night, make a list of three things that went well that day and things for which you are grateful.
- ❏ Have a special worry time well before bedtime, worry and put worries aside until the next worry time.
- ❏ Cry on purpose to release the tears that may be building up.
- ❏ Try a new recipe just for fun.
- ❏ Call a friend for a chat. If you must, talk five minutes about your ending relationship. Then go onto other topics, including asking about your friend's life.
- ❏ Join a support group.
- ❏ Find a counselor.
- ❏ Start journaling.
- ❏ Make a list of resentments and then tear up, burn or bury the list!
- ❏ Avoid hasty big decisions for a year or even more.
- ❏ Be cautious about making a big romantic commitment very quickly.
- ❏ Don't let the children become your entire life.
- ❏ Ask friends and family for help in finding resources you need.
- ❏ _____

TAKING CHARGE OF YOUR WELL-BEING
- ❏ Make a plan for the next month, and the month after that.
- ❏ Focus by creating a Must Do By _____ list and let the rest go for a while.
- ❏ Have a family meeting to go over issues that make running the house go more smoothly.
- ❏ Share chores with the children, even little chores and little children.
- ❏ Think hard and stick to the ground rules and guidelines you establish, even if the children complain.
- ❏ ALWAYS practice safe sex.
- ❏ _____

CHAPTER 5 – Emerging from Divorce

Just for Me

**It's time for you to do some things that are just for YOU!
Taking care of yourself – just for YOU – can mean many things.
Write comments on the lines below to consider how each item pertains to YOU.**

- Eat right, get enough rest and exercise. _____
_____

- Schedule a doctor's appointment for a check-up, no matter when you went last. _____
_____

- To avoid frustration or time crunches, be sure your car is in good working order. _____
_____

- Take care of little repairs in the house so they don't become big deals. _____
_____

- You will feel good if everyone in your household is fed and cared for. _____
_____

- Be creative with meals. Prepared foods are okay. _____
_____

- Try not to sweat the small stuff. _____
_____

- If you've never cooked, you have plenty of time to learn, little by little._____
_____

- Avoid forming bad habits because you are upset or feeling sorry for yourself. _____
_____

- Involve and nurture yourself through a variety of opportunities: house of worship, your community activities, yoga, meditation, music, books, volunteering, sports, classes, etc. _____
_____

- If you are feeling depressed for more than a few weeks, make an appointment with a therapist, counselor, or trusted friend. _____
_____

SECTION I – **The Process**

Routines

Many aspects of life will change for children of parents involved in a breakup, even the day-to-day rhythm of the household. Children benefit from having a predictable routine, particularly when so much in their life is changing. While the routines in each parent's household may not be the same, knowing what, when and where things are happening in each house will create a sense of stability for children. (Ideally, if both parents can adhere to the same routine, it is much easier on the children.)

What routines and time allotments will you have in your house?

Meals _____

_____

Bedtime_____

_____

Homework_____

_____

Television_____

_____

Computer and Other Electronics _____

_____

Text and Telephone_____

_____

Family Activities_____

_____

Household Chores_____

_____

Sleep-Overs _____

_____

Extra Curricular Activities _____

_____

Religious Services and Education_____

_____

Professional appointments (doctor, dentist, therapist, etc.) _____

_____

Other _____

_____

Accepting the Past

At some point, during or after the break up, it is time to accept the past, forgive the other person and yourself, and then move on with your new normal.

What have you accepted about the past? _____
_____
_____

What haven't you yet been able to accept about the past? _____
_____
_____

For what have you forgiven (not necessarily forgotten about) your ex-partner? _____
_____
_____

For what have you been unable to forgive your ex-partner? _____
_____
_____

For what have you forgiven yourself? _____
_____
_____

For what have you been unable to forgive yourself? _____
_____
_____

What have you been able to "let go"? _____
_____
_____

What have you been unable to "let go"? _____
_____
_____

How and what can you do to "let go"? _____
_____
_____

SECTION I – **The Process**

Letting Go Pointers

Letting go of the relationship as it used to be between you and your partner, is a critical part of getting on with your life. This means letting go of the anger and resentment, the guilt and regrets, and the dreams of what you hoped the relationship and your future would be.

The payoff for letting go is that you are free to explore and expand your new identity, make choices you may not have had before and get to know yourself in a different way.

Pointers about letting go:

- Anger is a secondary emotion, protecting us from feeling other more painful ones, like sadness, loneliness, etc.

- Remind yourself you did the best you could, knowing what you knew then.

- Allow yourself to grieve the losses you're experiencing.

- Try not to focus on the negative things your ex continues to do.

- Reach out to friends you really care about.

- Practice the serenity prayer.

- When tension about your ex starts to bubble over, take three deep easy breaths.

- Stay in the present.

- Limit the amount of time you talk about your ex.

- Set healthy boundaries with your ex.

- Notice your ex's behavior rather, but do not judge what's right or wrong about it.

- Consider what NOT letting go costs you in the short and long term.

- Accept that you and your ex co-created the negative as well as the positive parts of the relationship.

- Repeat: *"What my ex does or doesn't do is not my responsibility anymore."*

- Even if you haven't let go yet, act as if you have. ("fake it 'til you make it")

- Join a support group

CHAPTER **5 – Emerging from Divorce**

My New Life

Your life is probably changing dramatically, sometimes without your permission!

By taking a look at what is important to you – just you – you can feel more in charge of your new life. In the rate column, assign a number from 1 – 5 (1 = most important and 5 = least important). In the third column name something you can do in the next month to reflect these priorities.

IMPORTANT TO ME	RATE 1-5	ONE THING I CAN DO IN THE NEXT MONTH TO REFLECT THESE PRIORITIES.
Children		
Helping Others		
Finances		
Friendships		
Intellectual life		
My personal development		
Professional life		
Relationship with family		
Relationship with my ex		
Relationship with ex's family		
Religious / spiritual life		
Social life		
Other		
Other		
Other		
Other		

SECTION I – The Process

Single Again

When a committed relationship ends, you face many adjustments, one of which is being unattached. Being single at this point in your life is very different from being in your relationship. Whether it's been a few years or many, you may find the social scene very different from the one you knew before your committed relationship.

Here are some tips about approaching this part of your new life. Write your thoughts about each.

Give yourself time. Don't rush to begin dating, and certainly don't rush getting into a serious relationship. You need time to adjust to the loss of this relationship before you're ready to be emotionally close to someone new. _____

_____

Join some groups or new activities that interest you. _____

_____

Make new friends. You may find the network of friends you and your partner shared drifting away.

_____

_____

Making new friends who don't know your ex can give you a whole new support system and be eye-opening, as well. _____

_____

Think positively. If you think of yourself as a victim, that 's how others will see you. They are unlikely to want to spend a lot of time with you. As the song says, *put on a happy face*. You can do this, at least part of the time. _____

_____

The process of adjusting. Building a new social life involves exploring what's out there and what you want for yourself. Think of it as a research project. If one event doesn't go well, add it to your data base rather than drawing the conclusion that there's something wrong with you._____

_____

Becoming sexually active takes education and caution. You may want to be physically intimate after your breakup. That's a choice only you can make, but be sure you *thoroughly* understand how to have safe sex. Don't say yes to just anyone. _____

_____

In the Next Six Months

With so much happening in your life right now, you may feel overwhelmed with mixed feelings, new responsibilities, changing relationships, etc.

Thinking ahead and projecting where you would like to be six months from now can give you a sense of direction. Identifying your goals can be quite settling, and more importantly, can help bring those wishes to reality.

CRITERIA:

Consider your goals to be . . .

- *something you want*, not just what you think you should aim for.
- *specific* so you know what you are working toward.
- *realistic* enough to be doable in six months.
- *just yours*, so you are the one who can reach the goal yourself, without depending on anyone else.
- *focused* on what you want in your life right now.
- *achievable* – those you can put on a schedule and keep until you meet them.
- *worthy* – ones of which you will feel proud.
- *valuable* – goals you can celebrate when you have achieved them.

List 5 attainable goals that will meet the above criteria in the next six months.

1) _____
   _____
   _____

2) _____
   _____
   _____

3) _____
   _____
   _____

4) _____
   _____
   _____

5) _____
   _____
   _____

SECTION I – **The Process**

Recovery

It's difficult to predict how long it takes to recover from the ending of a committed relationship – and it may take longer than you think.

Recovered may mean the following to you:

- Stepping off the roller coaster of emotions.
- Accepting the end of the relationship as you've known it.
- Working out a more business-like way to deal with your ex.
- Feeling a new sense of yourself.

How will you know you've gotten through the emotional turmoil, uncertainty and intense attachment to the relationship?

Where are you now with each aspect of *recovery*?

- Feeling more stable emotionally. _____
  _____
  _____

- Accepting that the relationship is over. _____
  _____
  _____

- Finding a way that functions well to deal with your ex. _____
  _____
  _____

- Having a new, better sense of who you are. _____
  _____
  _____

Other ways you believe you will know that you are recovering.
_____
_____
_____
_____
_____

CHAPTER 5 – Emerging from Divorce

A Different Family but Still Family

One of the losses associated with the end of a committed relationship is the loss of family as you knew it. However, in this situation, what has happened is usually a change in the family, not its complete disappearance.

Place a check in the *True, False* or *Sometimes* boxes of the following statements.

ABOUT FAMILY	TRUE	FALSE	SOMETIMES
A family is a group of people who care for each other.			
A family is only a group of people who are related by blood or marriage.			
A family is born, not based on choice.			
A family is a place where two parents raise children together.			
Children can thrive in different kinds of families.			
When a single parent is raising children, it's not a real family.			
Couples raising children together should be legally married.			
There are many different ways to be a family.			
Parents should always stay together for the sake of the children,			
Children whose parents breakup never do well as adults.			
Stepchildren never develop close caring relationships.			
Children whose parents split up are more likely to do well when their parents don't put them in the middle.			
Children from parents of the same sex do not have a good life.			
Children of a blended family always have problems getting along.			
Same sex couples can raise healthy, well-behaved children.			
Adopted children are not real family.			
Blended families are usually troubled families.			
The best family is one with a breadwinner dad and homemaker mom.			
The nuclear family is a close-knit unit of dad, mom, and children – all in harmony.			
It is important for a family to have a stay-at-home mom.			

I believe a real family is one where _____

_____

_____

SECTION I – **The Process**

Coping with Now

Living as a single person after a committed relationship ends can seem overwhelming. So many things must be done – from the routine (like the laundry) – to the special tasks (like creating a new budget).

Suggestions for coping with your new life:

Be flexible

Use a journal to vent.

Find healthy distractions.

Don't try to do everything yourself.

Set priorities week by week and stick to the list.

Spend time with optimists, as well as sympathizers.

Take care of yourself even if you think you're too busy.

Explore interests you haven't had time to check out before.

Stick to your co-parenting agreement even if your ex doesn't.

Add twenty percent to the time you expect any task will take.

Give the gift of forgiveness to yourself and to your ex.

Tidy up, rearrange, organize, discard and make your space your own.

Avoid big decisions for a while once the legal end of the relationship is done.

Reach out to old friends but understand some of those relationships may drift away.

Put reminders of the relationship that has ended out of sight or in the children's space.

Learn self-soothing techniques like meditation, deep breathing, tai chi, massage, a hot bath, yoga and religious rituals, among others.

Do not touch, buy or keep a gun without very careful thought, guidance and safety education.

Avoid dangerous situations, like heavy drinking and/or drugging, unsafe sex, acting impulsively when angry, stalking, drinking when driving, etc.

Add suggestions to the above list . . .

_____

_____

_____

Old and New Traditions

One part of being in a family is having traditions that we can count on year after year, sometimes week after week. When a committed relationship ends, some traditions can't be maintained at all, while others may need to be changed. Creating NEW traditions is part of the task of rebuilding your life and that of your family.

In the Event column, add others in the blank spaces provided.
In the Old Traditions column fill in those traditions you and your family have always shared.
In the column on the right, note how you might modify an old tradition or create a new one to share.

If children are involved, ask them for their input. Fill in other personal events in the *other* rows.

EVENT	OLD TRADITIONS	NEW OR MODIFIED TRADITIONS
Birthdays		
Children's performances		
Family celebrations		
Family special day of the week dinner		
Get-togethers with friends		
Holidays		
Meals		
New Years		
School open houses and conferences		
Sports events		
Thanksgiving		
OTHER		
OTHER		

SECTION I – The Process

It's Been a Long Time Since I've Looked for a Job!

After the end of a committed relationship, you may need to find a job, perhaps for the first time in a long while. Thinking about your qualifications and what type of job might be available to you, may feel pretty overwhelming, especially early in the breakup.

While you might not have worked outside the home in a long time, or ever, you have worked and acquired skills and expertise you may not even recognize.

Find community resources, books and ideas on the Internet about resume writing, job interview and search skills, and other strategies for finding a job.

Networking: Make a list of 10 people to talk with about your resume. Brainstorm with them about a job search plan. Also, ask for names of others with whom you can talk.

1) _____   6) _____
2) _____   7) _____
3) _____   8) _____
4) _____   9) _____
5) _____   10) _____

Brainstorm available community resources.

_____
_____
_____
_____

Research **training or retraining programs** – local, state or non-profit agencies that can help evaluate the skills you already have or can train you.

_____
_____
_____
_____

A first step might be finding an entry level job to build up a work history, develop a sense of being in the workplace, and learn more about yourself as someone who can bring home a paycheck.

My Own Dreams

One of the losses we experience after the end of a committed relationship is the loss of our shared dreams. Finding new dreams can inspire, support and provide a sense of hope that we want and need as we shape our new lives. Here's a chance to reach for the stars - be impractical, unrealistic and have fun with secret old fantasies and new notions about what just might be possible, or even a little bit possible.

Complete the sentence starters below. Remember, no idea is too impractical. Have fun dreaming!

When I was a kid, I imagined _____
_____.

One adventure I'd love to have is _____
_____.

If I had no responsibilities I would _____
_____.

Now I have a chance to _____
_____.

My most secret desire is to _____
_____.

If I had all the money I could ever want, I would _____
_____.

I've always wanted to learn to _____
_____.

I want to be become _____
_____.

I want to help other people who _____
_____.

One way I can make the world a better place is _____
_____.

Rebuild My Social Life

The end of a committed relationship often involves the disruption of the social network we knew as a couple. Somehow, many friends seem to choose one side or the other. In other cases, couples may only socialize with other couples. Some partners of a couple may feel threatened by being close friends with an unattached person. If you're not partnered, you may or may not want to be with couples, depending on whether you feel comfortable.

While these experiences can be very upsetting, they also allow you to reshape your friendships. You may want friends who were not connected with the two of you. You may seek more people who share similar interests, perhaps people who are single, or other couples with whom you feel more comfortable.

The challenge may be to figure out how to make new connections. If you think about making friends rather than just meeting people to date, you may have better luck.

Some guidelines about adding to and building a social network you'll enjoy:

- Join a group or club that interests you.
- Attend events that interest you – even if you go alone – concerts, lectures, plays, museums, etc.
- Take up a new hobby or craft that involves being with other people – lessons, workshops, training programs.
- Volunteer at an organization whose focus you support.
- Get involved in a community activity (children's school, house of worship, political group, town events) where you can participate or join.

Identify what you might do to get yourself out of the house and meet new people.

- _____
- _____
- _____
- _____
- _____
- _____
- _____
- _____

CHAPTER 5 – **Emerging from Divorce**

Community Resources

COMMUNITY: a group of any size whose members reside in a specific locality, share government, have a common cultural and historical heritage or similar interests.

Joining, remaining in, or having a new involvement with a community of any type offers many advantages to the newly single. There are advantages and disadvantages of belonging to a community. Below, choose the communities that are a possibility for you and note the advantages and disadvantages of each. Add other interests in the blanks at the end of the list.

COMMUNITY	ADVANTAGES	DISADVANTAGES
Alumni association		
Book club		
Choir/orchestra/dance		
Civic group		
Computer group		
Continuing Ed. Courses		
Craft/hobby group		
Cultural group		
Dinner/show group		
Environmental group		
Exercise		
Financial group		
Friend of the library		
Game group		
Garden club		
Genealogy group		
House of worship		
Local school		
Nature group		
Neighborhood		
Photography club		
Political club		
Spiritual affiliation		
Sport team		
Support group		
Town events		
Travel group		
Wellness group		
Writer/poetry group		

SECTION I – **The Process**

Dating and the Internet

The Internet is a wonderful source of information about almost everything. It is also a fantastic tool to connect you with people you might not otherwise get to know. Like so many other new aspects of your life, you need to understand how online dating works so you can maximize the opportunities this resource can offer and stay safe.

Tips to keep in mind about on-line dating:

- Educate yourself. You will find a great many books and articles about Internet dating and lots of material on the Internet itself. Friends may be able to give you advice about the process, too.
- Check out more than one site to find one that seems to fit your needs and interests. Some sites have particular themes and focus on certain groups. Pay particular attention to the site's privacy policy.
- Look at profiles on the site(s) you select and define ideas about what you are looking for. More importantly, define clearly what you don't want. You can also get a sense of how you want to write your own profile by looking at how others describe themselves.
- Share enough information to give a picture of who you are and what your life is like, but do not reveal your entire life story. Be honest. Meeting someone under false pretenses means a disappointment for that person and ultimately a disappointment for you.
- Be specific about what you're looking for in another person, and more importantly, what you don't want. List the characteristics and traits important to you (family-minded, profession, religion, age, etc.).
- Be selective. You may need to sort through a number of contacts you connect with on an Internet dating site until you find a good match. Be sure the person you are in contact with has the qualities you consider worth your time.
- Stay anonymous. Use the site's message system until you become better acquainted. Some sites even have a voice message forwarding system which allows you to keep your phone number private. Give out your phone number ONLY when you feel comfortable and safe about having more direct contact.
- There is never a reason to share your Social Security Number, financial information or bank account numbers with someone you meet online. Do not stay in contact if this person asks for money.
- Once you've found someone you're interested in (and who is interested in you, too), talk on the phone to get to know each other better.
- If you both decide you want to meet, find and drive yourself to a neutral and open public place to meet, like a coffee shop or restaurant on a busy corner, preferably during the day. Be sure there will be other people both inside and outside the location you've chosen.
- Be cautious about consuming alcohol during a first meeting.
- Follow your instincts. If something doesn't seem right, leave. Be especially wary if this person asks you to do something you think is inappropriate and/or unsafe.
- Keep geography in mind. How far are you willing to travel to meet a new person or to date someone if you want to pursue a relationship?
- Be yourself. The goal is to find someone you feel is compatible with the "real you."

What other issues do you plan to consider when you explore Internet dating? _____
_____
_____

What other qualities do you plan to look for when you explore Internet dating prospects? _____
_____
_____

SECTION II

Practical Matters

SECTION II – Practical Matters

Sensible Steps

Exercises	Facilitator Tips	Page
What to Look for in a Legal Advisor	Review the list with participants and ask if any other questions should be included. If so, ask participants to write them on the back of the page. Follow up to monitor how the selection process is going.	137
What Documents Do I Need?	Divorce is a complicated administrative task as well as an emotional one. In a contentious divorce, one partner can make it difficult for the other by hiding important documents. Encourage participants to quietly gather whatever documents they can and to begin to do so sooner rather than later.	138
Trust but Verify	Note: the purpose of this exercise is to raise awareness of possible problems without damning everything. Expand the list with the participants. Discuss what the participants can to do verify without provoking a confrontation. Emphasize the positive aspects of the participants' answers, too.	139
Structure Your Financial Independence	Group can brainstorm other ways to become financially independent. Refer participants to the library or Internet to gather more information to bring back to the group at another session.	140
Separation Decisions	Encourage participants to answer these questions for themselves. After, participants can brainstorm how they might approach their ex-partners to develop a plan.	141
Who Gets the Sofa?	Ask for volunteers to each read one item. After each item is read, ask for input about how this item would work for them.	142
How to REALLY Separate	Brainstorm with the group other ways to establish boundaries. Ask participants to consider the best way to establish and keep new boundaries and to defuse the anger and tension when making plans.	143
Do I Need a Financial Adviser?	Understanding the tax consequences and long range financial impact of a settlement can be ignored during this highly emotional process. Emphasize that these matters are extremely important for participants to get the help they need to understand their agreement	144
Getting Connected	Refer to the glossary on pages 169-172 for items that may be unfamiliar.	145–146

SECTION II – Practical Matters

CHAPTER 6 – **Sensible Steps**

What to Look for in a Legal Advisor

Finding a legal advisor is one of the most important tasks when ending a committed relationship. In addition to evaluating a lawyer's professional qualifications, you'll want to evaluate the lawyer's personal style and approach. First, you need to have a consultation with any lawyer who might represent you. When you meet for the first time, consider the following personality issues and take notes!

Name of the lawyer _____

Did this person really listen to me?

My observations _____

_____

Did this person take time to understand my situation?

My observations _____

_____

Was the lawyer more interested in selling legal services than in listening to me?

My observations _____

_____

How accessible will this lawyer be when I need to be in contact?

My observations _____

_____

Did this person's assessment of my situation seem accurate to me?

My observations _____

_____

Did I hear legalese or did I hear understandable language during this conversation?

My observations _____

_____

Can this lawyer's style be adjusted to meet my goals?

My observations _____

_____

Did I get the sense that this lawyer could be conciliatory or aggressive as needed?

My observations _____

_____

What does this lawyer charge and can I afford this person?

_____

_____

SECTION II – **Practical Matters**

What Documents Do I Need?

Part of ending a committed relationship involves dividing up assets. This is the most important financial decision many people will ever make. You'll need to know your financial situation whether you use a lawyer and/or mediator. No matter what, who represents you, you need to understand your financial situation and your rights.

Below is a list of documents you may need to locate and photocopy or scan. Your lawyer or other advisor may add to the list, or might provide a standard list. If some of your assets are separate from those of your partner's, you will also want to copy that information, if you can.

- Bank statements (checking, savings, credit union, money market funds, CDs, cash)

- Business interests (family business, general partnerships, limited partnerships, receivables, payables, etc.)

- Current employment (recent pay stubs, total compensation, bonus history and expectations, etc.)

- Debts and liabilities (mortgage, deed, credit card statements, loans, promissory notes, liens, personal, student or family loans, equity lines of credit, etc.)

- Employee benefits (medical, COBRA, life, disability, etc.)

- Insurance policies (life, car, disability, personal umbrella, homeowners, etc.)

- Interest (earned from stocks, etc.)

- Investment statements (mutual funds, stocks, bonds, etc.)

- Personal property (estimated value of automobile, home furnishings, jewelry, furs, collections, boat, RV, etc.)

- Pre-nuptial agreement (if applicable)

- Real estate records (primary residence, vacation home, mortgage, liens, monthly payments, original purchase price, current value, etc.)

- Retirement plan statements (IRA, 401(k), pension plan, Keogh, employee stock ownership, annuity, profit-sharing, bonus, etc.)

- Safe deposit box (list of contents)

- Tax returns (past 5 years)

- Wills and trusts

- Other income and asset-related information

Trust but Verify

When you're ending a committed relationship, you have many details to work out – finances, housing, children, possessions, and many more. Because feelings can be so intense during this period, you (or your partner) may start intentionally or unintentionally misleading and/or stonewalling the other.

In the past, you may have had a trusting relationship about certain aspects of your life together. However, you would do well to check that your partner is honoring those commitments.

In this exercise, indicate with *yes* or *no* whether you trust your partner about various issues. In the last column indicate how it is going. Continue to monitor the process.

ISSUES	DO I TRUST MY PARTNER ABOUT THIS ISSUE?	HOW IS IT GOING?
Provide copies of documents you (and/or your lawyer) have requested.		
Pick up the children at the specified time.		
Move possessions out of the house if applicable.		
Keep appointments to talk to you about logistics.		
Put money into your bank account for you and/or children.		
Hired a moving van for the date promised.		
Promise to take care of you and/or the children without putting the commitment into the agreement.		
Divided up assets as promised.		
OTHER		
OTHER		
OTHER		
OTHER		
OTHER		

SECTION II – **Practical Matters**

Structure Your Financial Independence

Statistics show that after a breakup, women in particular suffer financially more than men. This may be due to their earning potential being less because of wage discrimination, interrupted careers to raise families, and/or courts being less sympathetic than formerly about women who have worked only in the home or part-time.

Ending a committed relationship in which finances have been shared may be the biggest financial transaction of your life and have an enormous impact immediately and in the future. Being aware of tasks you need to do is a key part of becoming financially independent.

Check the items that you have yet to do and add any others at the bottom of the list:

- ❑ Write up a realistic budget.
- ❑ List a clear set of income expectations.
- ❑ Set up personal credit and debit charge cards.
- ❑ Establish personal bank account(s).
- ❑ Change beneficiaries on insurance policies.
- ❑ Change beneficiaries on pension plans.
- ❑ Verify condition, loan or lease terms, points and outstanding tickets of car.
- ❑ List necessary house repairs.
- ❑ Note the liabilities you will assume if you keep the house.
- ❑ Calculate taxes you will owe as part of the settlement.
- ❑ Consider taxes you may owe on any profit from the sale of any property.
- ❑ Think about your fair share of marital assets.
- ❑ Have a plan to pay off debts.
- ❑ Consider expenses you can eliminate to balance, or begin to balance, your budget.
- ❑ See a vocational counselor for guidance on improving your career-related skills.
- ❑ Create an income and expense form and update monthly.
- ❑ List new medical expenses and monthly premiums if you and/or your children are no longer covered under your partner's medical plans.
- ❑ Have a plan to save for your retirement regardless of your age.
- ❑ Talk to a financial planner about your situation if needed.
- ❑ Verify beneficiaries on your will and living will documents.
- ❑ Verify ownership designation on stocks, bonds, etc.
- ❑ Open a new separate safety deposit bank box.
- ❑ _____
- ❑ _____
- ❑ _____

Being aware of tasks you need to do is a key part of becoming financially independent.

Separation Decisions

Deciding to separate is an enormous step. Ideally, it involves careful planning, preparation and sensitivity, whether the partners see this as a trial separation or the first step in ending the relationship. Think carefully through the process in a step-by-step way, You might avoid at least some of the heartache that breaking up inevitably causes, both for the partners and the children. Remember, your final agreement will not necessarily be the same as your separation agreement.

Issues to discuss with your partner.

- How long will the separation be?
- Is the separation a chance to think things through (a trial separation) or definitely the first step toward finalizing the end of the commitment to each other?
- Most important, how, when and where will the children be told and by whom (together whenever possible)?
- What message should be delivered to the children about the nature of the separation (trial, first step toward divorce, other?)
- Publicize the decision? Who will be informed, by whom and when?
- What is the family calendar during the separation period, what to do and with whom? (Children's activities, vacations, visits with relatives, holiday and special occasion celebrations, etc.)
- How will already-planned social commitments be handled? How about new invitations?
- How will finances work? Who will pay the bills, mortgage, car lease, utilities, etc., during this period? What about child support, allowances, purchases for children, etc.?
- What furniture and other household items will the partner who is moving out take?
- Consider a couples' therapist? Individual therapists?
- How frequently and at what time should the partners talk on the phone?
- When, where and how will the partner no longer living with the kids see or talk with them?
- Are the expectations and plans about dating during this period explicit, so both parties know what to expect?
- Have specific plans been made for where the partner who is moving out be living? Timing? Is there room for the children to stay?
- Can the children choose where to live?
- Agree to respect each other's privacy - no drive-bys, tracking phone calls, quizzing kids, checking with friends and family about the other's activities.
- Schedule meetings for partners in a public place or a counselor's or mediator's office to discuss the process, further plans, etc.

SECTION II – Practical Matters

Who Gets the Sofa?

Dividing up household items can be challenging, especially if you both want the same item. Setting up an orderly process can help eliminate some of the struggles.

GUIDELINES TO CONSIDER

1. **Heirlooms** automatically go the person whose family it came from.

2. **Gifts** received from one side of the family usually go to the person whose family gave the gift.

3. **Set aside the things that need to stay** where the children are spending most of their time (if applicable). Recognize that the items children care most about are likely to go back and forth with them from one house to another.

4. **Begin by labeling** the items that you both clearly agree belong to one or the other.

5. **Make a list**, room by room, of items in the household.

6. **Agree on a process that each of you see as fair.** One way might be to take turns, one after the other, flipping a coin to see who starts.

7. **If finances are important,** each of you can put a dollar amount next to each item. Average the two estimates. Choose. Check to see if the two amounts add up to about the same amount. Adjust as needed by swapping one item for another or paying the difference. You can try to pick items of comparable value, but it might be easier to total your choice and then adjust.

8. **Set aside items you can't agree on.** Each of you can come back perhaps with a suggestion on how to resolve this disagreement. If not, perhaps a third party, such as a mediator, can help resolve the issue. An appraiser can help if items are financially rather than sentimentally valuable. If all else fails, you can always flip a coin.

IF YOU CAN'T AGREE

**The court could decide without taking sentimental meaning into account.
Lawyers could negotiate for each of you at considerable expense.
You still may not be satisfied with the results.**

How to REALLY Separate

Ending a committed relationship involves disentangling your life from that of your partner. You might not have thought about how interconnected you and your partner are in your day-to-day very practical routines. If you have children, you will continue to have some sort of relationship for the rest of your lives.

Experts say establishing new, clear boundaries in your relationship with your partner is critical as you create a new relationship reflecting the break-up. Having a newly defined relationship is part of having a new, healthy life for yourself.

To create new, healthy boundaries . . .

- eliminate involvement with each other except in your parenting roles.
- set up a schedule of how and when you'll be in touch (phone, email, texting).
- resist and discourage contact outside of the agreed upon schedule.
- avoid asking or answering personal questions, e.g., *"Are you dating?"* or *"Are you seeing a counselor?"*
- forgo asking friends and relatives personal questions about your partner.
- keep the schedule you've established for seeing and talking to the children, at least until things settle down.
- refrain from asking your partner to help with household tasks, including laundry, bill paying, car maintenance, house repairs.
- mail support payments just as you would with any other bill you pay with a check.
- have pre-arranged meetings in public places to discuss practicalities, without discussing personal problems and issues.
- write agreements you reach so you are both clear about what you've decided together.
- talk about only current concerns and plans, not about the past.
- _____
- _____
- _____
- _____
- _____

SECTION II – Practical Matters

Do I Need a Financial Advisor?

It is imperative to understand the tax consequences and long-term impact of the financial agreement you make with your partner. Your lawyer may be able to develop a strategy for your financial negotiations and help you understand the tax consequences of your decisions. Nonetheless, you might find the services of one or more financial advisors important during the process of dividing up assets.

Which particular adviser you need depends on the complexity of your situation. Your lawyer should be able to tell you if a financial advisor should also work on your case, and which type of advisor you need.

Take a look at the list of issues and check either the yes or no column.

ISSUES	YES	NO
We have complicated joint assets (property, investment portfolio, business interests, retirement plans, etc.).		
It is possible that my partner is hiding some of our joint assets.		
I believe that a financial planner, accountant or investment adviser would have my best interests in mind.		
I am ready to make decisions about my assets.		
I do not have a complete picture of the financial issues I will have after we have settled.		
I already know someone I can trust who knows a lot about finances.		
My lawyer thinks I need other financial advisers during the negotiations.		
I have left all the money matters to my partner.		
I have no idea about how to arrive at, or ask for, a settlement.		
I don't understand how my partner's pension works.		
I need help with tax consequences.		

"Yes" answers suggest consulting with a financial person, or checking with your attorney about these issues.

CHAPTER **6 – Sensible Steps**

Getting Connected

Family and friends can be excellent practical as well as emotional supports during the end of a committed relationship. As you move forward with the process of breaking up, you may not know how to start the search for qualified advisors. Asking people you know is a good place to begin. If they do not have any suggestions, they may know someone who does.

Fill in the names of people who might know and/or be able to refer you to the following resources:

Three people you can ask for referrals to a family law attorney:

1 _____
2 _____
3 _____

Three people you can ask for referrals to a mediator:

1 _____
2 _____
3 _____

Three people you can ask for referrals to a financial planner:

1 _____
2 _____
3 _____

Three people you can ask for referrals to a tax lawyer and/or accountant:

1 _____
2 _____
3 _____

(Continued on the next page)

SECTION II – **Practical Matters**

Getting Connected (Continued)

Three people you can ask for referrals to a real estate agent:

1. _____
2. _____
3. _____

Three people you can ask for referrals to a business appraiser:

1. _____
2. _____
3. _____

Three people you can ask for referrals to a parenting "coordinator" (a person who helps couples work out a parenting agreement):

1. _____
2. _____
3. _____

Three people you can ask for referrals to a counselor/therapist specializing in work with children and/or families:

1. _____
2. _____
3. _____

Other professions whose expertise you might need:

1. _____
2. _____
3. _____

CHAPTER 7 – The Negotiations

The Negotiations

Exercises	Facilitator Tips	Page
Questions to Ask a Lawyer	Ask participants if they had any other questions and suggest that they write those questions on the back of the pages. Emphasize the importance of taking notes during the meeting. You might want to recommend that they bring a trusted confidant to the meeting with them as a second set of ears.	149–150
What Can a Lawyer Do for Me?	Go around the room and ask each participant to read an item. After each is read, discuss with the group.	151
Answers I Need	Set this up as a group exercise. Role-play with participants asking questions. Examples: ▪ Documentation needed (tax returns) ▪ Immediate money arrangements (joint bank statements, bills, support payments) ▪ What to expect in the process (how long, steps involved) ▪ Other advisors needed (accountant, mediator)	152–153
Is Mediation Right for Us?	Many jurisdictions require divorcing parties to see a mediator briefly before finalizing their agreement. Encourage participants to evaluate if a longer mediation process can lessen the hostility and tension that can get in the way of a fair and efficient process and leave a residue of resentment behind.	154
Co-Parenting Agreements	After handout is completed ask participants to share items with which they believe their partner will disagree.	155–156
Financial Separation	Discuss the importance of establishing one's own credit and limiting liability for any debts their partner might incur after the decision to separate has been made. Follow up from time to time to check on progress being made.	157
What's it Going to Cost Me?	Ask the group to brainstorm other items that need to be included in estimating the yearly expenses as well as the expenses that would be incurred if starting another household. Mention how useful a computer-based budgeting program can be.	158
How Long is this Going to Take?	Encourage participants to discuss whether they want the process to go as quickly as possible. Then explore the advantages and disadvantages of speeding it up or slowing down. NOTE: Experts recommend not rushing to settle.	159
What IF?	Encourage participants to do homework on the issues raised on this handout, especially the taxes and future value of the financial offers.	160

SECTION II – Practical Matters

CHAPTER 7 – **The Negotiations**

Questions to Ask a Lawyer

Lawyers, like physicians, have specialties. Lawyers who work with clients wanting to end a committed relationship legally specialize in family/divorce law. You can often get recommendations about lawyers from friends, family and the local bar association.

Here's a list of questions you might want to ask a lawyer with whom you are consulting. Take these pages with you when you go to your first appointment with an attorney. Now, check those below you wish to ask, and during your consultation, write the responses on the lines next to each question.

❏ How much experience have you had practicing family law?
_____
_____
_____

❏ What determines which cases go to court or are settled out of court?
_____
_____
_____

❏ Who else in your office would be working with my case?
_____
_____
_____

❏ How quickly can I expect a phone call to be returned?
_____
_____
_____

❏ Who is likely to return my calls?
_____
_____
_____

❏ Can you explain your fee structure?
_____
_____
_____

(Continued on the next page)

SECTION II – **Practical Matters**

Questions to Ask a Lawyer *(Continued)*

❏ May I have a copy of the attorney-client agreement to review?
_____
_____

❏ What are your thoughts about using a mediator in my situation?
_____
_____

❏ Do you do mediation?
_____
_____

❏ Who normally helps the parties work out a co-parenting agreement?
_____
_____

❏ Do you believe that children should ever testify in a divorce trial?
_____
_____

❏ What do you think your reputation is with other family law attorneys?
_____
_____

❏ How much input will I have about the way the case moves forward?
_____
_____

❏ Have you ever been disciplined by the state bar?
_____
_____

❏ Other
_____
_____

What Can a Lawyer Do for Me?

A lawyer can try to help . . .

- with paperwork.

- deal with the court so you don't need to.

- negotiate in trying to settle the case.

- review a mediated agreement.

- figure out what you and your partner each owned before the break up and since.

- sort out your assets and debts, especially if they are complicated.

- act to protect you and the children if there is a problem with any type of abuse.

- if your partner is being dishonest or vindictive and you can't cope with it.

- act to protect you and the children if your partner abuses drugs or alcohol.

- keep the process going if and when your partner is impossible to talk to or deal with.

- negotiate with an aggressive opposing attorney.

- be sure that all of both of your assets are being accounted for.

- track down your partner's assets if they are hidden.

- recognize that if your partner has a lawyer, you need one of your own.

- coordinate with the other advisors.

SECTION **II – Practical Matters**

Answers I Need

For many of us, dealing with lawyers, financial advisors, mediators, parenting coordinators and others is a new and scary world. Having a list of questions to ask when you first consult with one or more of these professionals can help reduce your fears. Keep in mind, even if we know what to ask, it's difficult to remember every detail of the answers we receive. Write the responses you receive from the questions you ask.

Questions I have about . . .

Children _____
_____
_____
_____
_____

Temporary Living Arrangements _____
_____
_____
_____
_____

Cost of Advisors' Services _____
_____
_____
_____
_____

Documentation Needed _____
_____
_____
_____
_____

(Continued on the next page)

CHAPTER 7 – **The Negotiations**

Answers I Need *(Continued)*

Immediate Money Arrangement _____

_____

_____

_____

_____

What to Expect in the Process _____

_____

_____

_____

_____

Separation Agreement Terms _____

_____

_____

_____

_____

Other Advisors Needed _____

_____

_____

_____

_____

Other Issues _____

_____

_____

_____

_____

SECTION II – **Practical Matters**

Is Mediation Right for Us?

Mediation is a process designed to help partners who are ending a committed relationship work through the wide range of decisions that need to be made. In many locations, some mediation is required by the courts before a divorce can be finalized.

A trained mediator can help you negotiate for yourselves rather than each having lawyers negotiate for you. Keep in mind that mediation doesn't mean you should each not have a lawyer. Experts advise each partner to hire a lawyer to review the mediated agreement. Mediation is usually less expensive than hiring two lawyers for the entire process.

These questions can help you decide if mediation is right for you.

1. How do you and your partner stand up for yourselves or does one of you avoid confrontation at all costs? _____
_____

2. In what way are both of you ready to accept the fact that you won't be getting back together? _____
_____

3. If there is any history of any type of abuse in this relationship, what is your safety plan? _____
_____

4. Are you willing to share your complete financial information and do you trust your partner to do so? If not, what will you do? _____
_____
_____

5. How serious are you both about wanting to reach an agreement that's fair for both of you? _____
_____

6. How much do you want your partner to continue to have a relationship with your children? _____
_____

7. What is really important in this process? _____
_____
_____

8. How determined are you both to give mediation a fair chance before looking for other alternatives? _____
_____

CHAPTER 7 – **The Negotiations**

Co-Parenting Agreements

When children are involved in a breakup, the court requires a plan detailing how children will be cared for afterwards. Professionals, lawyers and mediators are available to work with a couple to develop a co-parenting plan. Usually these plans are very specific and spell out who does what, when and where. The more detailed the plan, the less room there is for disagreements in the future.

Look at the following items and write what you want in the co-parenting agreement. Keep in mind, your partner may have very different ideas.

Where, when and with whom will the children live? _____
_____
_____

What will be the schedule for time with each parent during a school week and the weekend? _____
_____
_____

How will the children get from place to place (school, other parent, dentist, etc.) _____
_____
_____

How will medical and dental decisions be made? _____
_____
_____

How will holidays, vacations and celebrations be divided up? _____
_____
_____

For how long and where can a parent take a child on vacation? _____
_____
_____

What consistent rules for each home can be agreed to? _____
_____
_____

(Continued on the next page)

SECTION II – **Practical Matters**

Co-Parenting Agreements *(Continued)*

Who will go to teacher conferences? _____

_____

_____

Who will handle school issues? _____

_____

_____

How will children continue to have contact with your partner's extended family? _____

_____

_____

What extra curricular activities will continue? _____

_____

_____

How will school, camp, college expenses be paid? _____

_____

_____

When and how will the children be in touch with your partner when they are with you? _____

_____

_____

When and how will the children be in touch with you when they are with your partner? _____

_____

_____

How will the agreement be changed as circumstances change? _____

_____

_____

How will disagreements about parenting be resolved? _____

_____

_____

CHAPTER **7 – The Negotiations**

Financial Separation

One very complicated aspect of committed relationships is often the couple's finances. Experts recommend separating finances as soon as a separation is about to happen or already underway. Waiting until a formal separation agreement or breakup becomes final is generally a poor strategy.

Place a check in the boxes of the following list of items that apply to you if your finances are combined with your ex-partner. Make this your *To Do* list.

❑ Prepare an inventory of all bank accounts, credit cards, loans, etc., that are in both names.

❑ Open your own bank account.

❑ Arrange for direct deposit of your pay check to your personal bank account.

❑ Notify credit card companies that you want to open your own credit card.

❑ Instruct credit card companies to take your name off of any joint credit card accounts.

❑ Inform credit card companies in writing that you are not responsible for any charges your partner might make from this date forward.

❑ Close joint credit lines (such as line of credit with your bank, or related to your mortgage).

❑ Contact three major credit bureaus explaining you are setting up your own credit and want to separate your credit rating from your partner's.

❑ Change beneficiary on life insurance, pension, retirement and investment accounts, and wills, living wills and trusts.

❑ Change the passwords of every online account, including social media and professional online groups.

Is there anything else you need to do for you financial separation?

❑ _____

❑ _____

❑ _____

❑ _____

Keep in mind:

- Obtain written documentation of every change.

- You are responsible for any debts with both your names on the documents up until the ime you notify the lender or credit card company that you will no longer be responsible for any further debts.

- The division of mortgage liabilities can only be resolved as part of a formal agreement, such as a divorce decree.

- As in all financial matters, make a copy of every document you send and note the *time, date and name of company representatives.*

SECTION II – Practical Matters

What's it Going to Cost Me?

You and your partner probably have an economic deal, whether you've thought of it that way or not. A change in finances, often a significant one, is almost always a central part of ending a committed relationship.

It is very important to document your expenses from the past year.

EXPENSES	NEED TO DO IT	DONE	N/A
Child care			
Children's extra activities			
Children's school expenses			
Education			
Entertainment			
Food (home, eating out, coffee shop, etc.)			
Gifts			
Health care (physical, self-care, club, exercise)			
Home expenses (repairs, utilities, supplies, yard, cleaning)			
Interest on loans and credit card payments			
Loans			
Medical and dental premiums and co-pays			
Mortgage			
Pet care			
Rent			
Savings, stocks, etc.			
Transportation (public transportation and vehicle expenses)			
Travel			
Utilities			
Wearing apparel			

If it applies to you, estimate the cost of setting up another household.

How Long is This Going to Take?

Legally ending a committed relationship can take what seems to be forever. The actual time depends on a number of factors. You can influence the process somewhat, but not entirely. Below are some factors that may have an impact on the pace of the process. Comment on how each item applies in your situation.

The longer the relationship has gone on, the longer it may take to agree on who gets what, for how long and in what form.
_____
_____

Making decisions about the children.
_____
_____

Either partner fighting the formal end of the relationship every step of the way.
_____
_____

One partner not competent to make personal decisions.
_____
_____

One partner abandoned the household and family.
_____
_____

One or both partners focusing only on winning and unwilling to compromise.
_____
_____

Complicated finances.
_____
_____

The style of the attorneys representing each party.
_____
_____

SECTION II – **Practical Matters**

What IF?

Sometimes when we are in the midst of a personal crisis, such as the end of a committed relationship, we lose sight of how our needs, requirements and wants may change. While we know that our children will be growing and changing, we might forget that we, too, will be different over time.

Thinking ahead may help you avoid potential problems and plan more effectively for your future.

Below are some what if's to think about. Check the situations that apply to you and elaborate below on ways you can recognize these potential changes and build them into your negotiations.

❑ What if I decide to go back to school to improve my career opportunities?
_____
_____

❑ What if I can't afford to keep the house, as much as I might want to? _____
_____
_____

❑ What if I don't understand the long-term implications of the settlement I'm being offered? _____
_____
_____

❑ What if I want to move away with my children? _____
_____
_____

❑ What if I don't trust my partner to honor the agreements we make about our finances, property and children? _____
_____
_____

❑ What if I need to get a job when I haven't worked outside the home for a long time?_____
_____
_____

❑ What if I don't understand the tax implications of the settlement I'm being offered?_____
_____
_____

❑ What if I can get support for the children only until they are 18 years old and then I'm on my own?
_____
_____

CHAPTER 8 – **Understanding the Financial Divorce**

Understanding the Financial Divorce

Exercises	Facilitator Tips	Page

Prepare for the Financial Divorce	Examples:
	    Payments (child support, on-going expenses, increases in agreed upon expenses, etc.)
	    Future expenses (college tuition, orthodontia)
	    Titles (property, car, trusts)
		163

My Thoughts about Money	Ask for volunteers to share their responses to the last prompt.	164
Where to Learn More about Money	Ask the participants to complete the sentence prompts the best they can. After handouts are completed, lead a discussion of each prompt.	165
TIPS for Analyzing Options	Ask participants to each read a bulleted point. After each one, lead a discussion of each item. After volunteers have read each tip, discuss how they may be applicable to them. Then brainstorm other tips, and ask participants to write those they think would be helpful, on the bulleted lines at the bottom of the page.	166
Checklist of Settlement Issues	Encourage participants to cross off any items that are not applicable to their situation, and to add any items not listed.	167

SECTION II – Practical Matters

CHAPTER 8 – Understanding the Financial Divorce

Prepare for the Financial Divorce

Division of property during a break up involves more than who gets the DVDs. When you've shared a life, usually your financial affairs are intermingled as well.

To prepared for each phase of the financial divorce indicate what you need to do, and how you will do it. If you have already taken care of the task, place a check in the box.

The financial facts:
- ❑ Identify all assets _____
- ❑ Detail debts_____
- ❑ Clarify current budget_____
- ❑ Project future expenses _____
- ❑ Create and document temporary financial agreement _____

Separate your assets and debts – which are yours, which are your partners' and which you share:
- ❑ Identify your assets _____
- ❑ Detail your debts*_____
- ❑ Project future expenses for your separate household _____

What you need to understand during negotiations:
- ❑ Tax implications of proposed settlement _____
- ❑ Who is responsible for each debt _____
- ❑ What the impact of inflation could be on the settlement _____
- ❑ The short- and long-term costs of keeping the house _____

Be specific and document, document, document!
- ❑ The temporary settlement_____
- ❑ The final settlement_____
- ❑ Lump sum and periodic payments _____

Change documents to reflect the divorce:
- ❑ Beneficiary designations_____
- ❑ Separate bank accounts _____
- ❑ Titles to property held jointly_____
- ❑ Your will_____
- ❑ Advance health care directives_____
- ❑ Power of attorney_____
- ❑ Credit cards _____
- ❑ Notify credit rating service that your credit is separate from your partner's _____
- ❑ Other: _____

_____
_____

*Remember you and your partner are both liable for your combined debts until a financial settlement is final.

SECTION **II – Practical Matters**

My Thoughts about Money

We all have ideas about money that influence how we approach financial negotiations, spend money, think about the role of money in our lives, and more.

Complete the following sentences:

The message I got from my mother about money _____
_____

The message I got from my father about money _____
_____

Other money messages I received growing up _____
_____

I feel capable of handling money _____
_____

I worry about the responsibility of managing my own finances _____
_____

In managing money, I _____
_____

I can learn more about handling money by _____
_____

My money role in my relationship _____
_____

The way I now need to deal with money _____
_____

The most important lesson about money for children to learn _____
_____

Now that I'm in charge of my own finances, I _____
_____

CHAPTER 8 – **Understanding the Financial Divorce**

Where to Learn More about Money

You may now be responsible for your own finances, either for the first time, or after a long time of sharing your financial affairs with your partner.

One important way of dealing with changing financial responsibilities is to learn more about money matters. Complete the following sentences.

My bank can help me by _____
_____
_____.

The human resources department at the workplace can help me by _____
_____
_____.

My local library might have useful information, like _____
_____
_____.

I could take a course about money at _____
_____
_____.

_____ knows a lot about _____
_____
_____.

I need help with _____
_____
_____.

I will be better off financially when I know more about _____
_____
_____.

Other money issues I should understand better include _____
_____
_____.

TIPS for Analyzing Options

It may be challenging to think logically and practically about finances when our emotions are so intense. In the end, it boils down to numbers – dollars and cents.

Take a look at the following tips. Think about how they fit into your situation.

- Be prepared for bad scenes, high levels of tension and possible threats.

- Develop a work plan for gathering the information you need to make an informed decision about the offers your partner may make. A work plan can help you avoid feeling overwhelmed by all the information you need to gather.

- Ask questions about the alternatives and long-term impact of any financial decisions you're facing.

- Don't let your eagerness to get it done already interfere with giving negotiations the time needed to work through each of the challenging steps to reach an agreement.

- Make sure you understand the tax implications of any decision you may make. Always ask, "What will my tax liability be if I . . . ?"

- Before you sign anything, be sure you consult an expert – accountant, lawyer, consumer credit counselor, financial planner, banker – who can give you objective advice.

- Even if you and your partner both want a friendly negotiation, keep in mind that you are NOT on the same side. You have different interests and goals that may be contrary to one another.

- Think ahead. Consider the impact of any offer over time – in one year, two, five and ten years, when the kids are going off to college, when they are independent.

- Become financially intelligent – ask, study, verify and ask some more.

- Slow down, slow down, slow down until you know you have all the facts and believe you understand the short and long range implications of what you have decided.

Add Other Tips:

- _____
- _____
- _____
- _____
- _____

CHAPTER **8 – Understanding the Financial Divorce**

Checklist of Settlement Issues

When you're working to reach a settlement at the end of a committed relationship, you have many financial issues to consider. This chart can remind you of specific information you need. *(Who holds the title, beneficiary, fair market value, cash amount, after tax value, etc.?)*

ASSETS	I NEED TO FIND OUT THE FOLLOWING INFORMATION:
House – Primary Residence	
House – Other home(s)	
Time Share(s)	
Retirement Plan(s)	
Investments	
Cash	
Bank Account Balances	
Business Ownership	
Limited Partnerships	
Personal Property	
Insurance Policies	
OTHER	
OTHER	
LIABILITIES (DEBTS)	
Mortgage – Principal	
Mortgage – Balance	
Mortgage – Monthly payments	
Mortgage – Time Share(s)	
Car Loan	
Car Loan	
Student Loan	
Student Loan	
Prior Alimony Payment	
Lease Obligation(s)	
Outstanding Loan(s)	
Line(s) of Credit	
Credit Card Balance	
Credit Card Balance	
IOUs	
OTHER	
OTHER	

© 2013 WHOLE PERSON ASSOCIATES, 210 WEST MICHIGAN ST., DULUTH MN 55802-1908 • 800-247-6789

SECTION II – Practical Matters

Breaking Up Is Hard to Do
Glossary of Terms

Often, in divorce proceedings and breakups, many terms that come up may be confusing or unfamiliar. The purpose of this glossary is to provide a quick description of some legal and financial terms as they apply to divorce and breakups.

These definitions are intended to be informational only and not for the purpose of providing legal or financial advice.

Actuary
A person who calculates the current value of future pension payments.

Alimony
A payment made to one's spouse or former spouse decided by a court.

Annuity
A specific payment for a specific period or until death, based on premiums paid.

Appraisal
An evaluation of the value of a business and other property prepared by a professional who specializes in assessing the value of that kind of asset.

Assets
Items of ownership able to be converted to cash.

Balloon Payment
A large payment that concludes a series of smaller payments.

Bankruptcy
A legal proceeding when one demonstrates the inability to pay debts.

Bond
An investment in which the seller agrees to pay a specific amount for a specific period of time.

Child Support
Money paid for the care of one's minor child, usually during a separation or after a divorce.

COBRA
Consolidated Omnibus Budget Reconciliation Act. Federal law that specifies rights to continued health care coverage when eligibility for coverage would otherwise end.

COLA
Cost Of Living Adjustment that reflects the rising cost due to inflation.

Community Property
Property that belongs to both partners, usually during marriage. A law may differ from state to state. In some states, domestic partners may have rights to community property.

Co-parenting Agreement
Required by courts issuing a divorce decree. Requires a specific plan detailing where a minor child will live, spend vacations, holidays, celebrations and many other aspects of shared parenting responsibilities.

Credit
Payment history that can determine one's responsibility and risk in regard to lenders or charge cards.

Glossary of Terms

Custody
A legal term that specifies who makes decisions for a child's welfare, where the child will live and the duty of the parent to care for the child's welfare and education. *Legal* and *physical* custody may be different. State laws may differ.

Debt
Something that is owed. During a committed relationship, the debts of one partner may be considered the other partner's responsibility.

Defined Benefits Plan
A pension plan that pays a specific amount when requirements are met, often related to length of service and age. Spouses have certain rights to pension payments.

Defined Contribution Plan
A pension plan that accumulates money over time, usually contributed by an employer and employee. Spouses have certain rights to payouts from the plan.

Deposition
Testimony given under oath, outside of court. Often used as a way to gather evidence in a contested divorce.

Divorce
A legal proceeding that ends the legal duties and responsibilities of a marriage. Laws governing divorce differ from state to state and from country to country.

Equity
The monetary value of a property or business minus any amount owed.

Estate Plan
A series of documents which provides instructions and declarations regarding how assets should be distributed upon death or incapacity.

Garnishment of Wages
A court-ordered amount of money withheld from wages. Sometimes necessary when child support and/or alimony payments have not been made as specified by a separation agreement or divorce decree.

Health Insurance
Medical coverage. An important consideration in separation agreements and divorce negotiations.

Inflation
Price and cost of living increases.

Investments
Money used to get a profitable return. Can include stocks, bonds, property and other items expected to grow in value.

IRA
Individual Retirement Account. Designed to be used to fund retirement. Depending on state law, spouses may have rights to IRA holdings at the time of divorce.

IRS
Internal Revenue Service. The Federal taxing entity that can tax what money one receives as a result of a separation agreement or divorce.

Joint Account
Bank or investment accounts over which both signatories have authority.

Glossary of Terms

Joint Tax Returns
Reporting income together to the IRS and other government entities. Couples who file jointly are responsible for one hundred percent of the tax due as well as share any related penalties and interest if the other partner does not pay his/her share. A very important aspect of a divorce agreement. It is to both partners' benefit to clearly state in the agreement who is responsible for what when it comes to taxes.

Liens
A legal claim on property often used to secure the payment of a debt. Can be part of what is owed on a house or other property.

Loans
Something lent or furnished on condition of being returned that can be the responsibility of both partners.

Marital Debts
Generally both partners are responsible for repayment on anything owed during a committed relationship, depending on state law.

Marital Property
Property acquired usually during a marriage to which both partners may have rights. In some states, may also apply to domestic partners.

Mediation
A process that can help resolve disagreements without lawyers advocating for one side or the other. A mediated agreement should be reviewed by the lawyer of each party.

Memorandum of Understanding
A document that details what has been agreed to, often the final step in mediation. Can be submitted to a court as part of the filing for divorce.

Money Market Funds
An investment in a pool of funds, such as stocks, bonds and other assets. Also called mutual funds.

Mortgages
Amounts loaned on property, most commonly on a house, but can be for other property as well.

Net Worth
What an individual or couple is worth after all debts have been deducted from their assets.

Options
The right to purchase stock for a particular price after a specific date. Can be an asset that a spouse has certain rights to.

Parental Rights
Specified by law and may vary from state to state.

Pension Plan
A benefit usually sponsored by an employer that pays a benefit based on specific rules and federal law. Spouses may have certain rights to pension plan benefits earned during the marriage.

Prenuptial Agreement
A contract, entered into prior to a committed relationship, specifying what will happen financially if the relationship ends or if there is a death.

Glossary of Terms

Present Value
Current value of a future payout. May be applicable to a division of pension benefits payable at a later date. Often determined by an actuary or accountant.

Promissory Notes
A promise to make future payments. Often used to buy out a spouse's share of a jointly-owned business, house or other property.

Rental Property
When owned by both partners or acquired during a marriage, an asset that may be part of the financial negctiation.

Rollover
Transferring assets from one tax-deferred account to another. Used when a payment is made from a pension plan to avoid paying federal income taxes or penalties at the time of the transfer.

Separation
Can be informal or a legally-binding agreement. Needs to address financial arrangements and parenting issues.

Social Security Benefits
Eligibility for payments based on former spouse's Social Security record if

they were married for a period of time and under circumstances specified by federal law.

Stocks
Shares in a company. Value may change over time. Important to fix date of valuing the stock in negotiating a financial settlement.

Subpoenas
A court order to produce certain information, or participate in legal proceedings. Not honoring the subpoena, withholding or falsifying information is considered contempt of court and is punishable by a fine or jail, or both.

Tax Basis
The amount property is worth after all associated expenses and debts have been subtracted. Important in dividing assets.

Tax Returns
Reports of income and deductions to federal, state and local governments.

Temporary Separation
Either a written or verbal agreement to live apart. Key issues to negotiate include financial arrangements and parenting activities.

Temporary Support Agreement
An agreement regarding finances before a divorce agreement has been reached. Can be modified in the final agreement.

Visitation
Arrangements for spending time with the parent with whom the children don't live. May be part of a parenting agreement.

Book References

The following list includes books that both facilitators and participants may find help raise awareness of important issues, find answers to many questions and review suggestions about moving through the breaking-up process.

Many of these references specifically address issues associated with ending a marriage through divorce. Some, despite the title, may be helpful for those in a committed relationship who have not married or been joined in a civil union.

The Internet is also a valuable resource for articles, tips and finding organizations that address specific issues associated with breaking up.

Clapp, Genevieve
Divorce & New Beginnings: An Authoritative Guide to Recovery and Growth, Solo Parenting, and Stepfamilies

Doskow, Emily
Nolo's Essential Guide to Divorce

Everett, Craig & Everett Sandra
Healthy Divorce: For Parents and Children – An Original, Clinically Proven Program for Working Through the Fourteen Stages of Separation, Divorce and Remarriage

Green, Janice
Divorce After 50: Your Guide to Unique Legal and Financial Challenges

Lyster, Mimi E.
Child Custody: Building Parenting Agreements that Work

Sherman, Ed
Divorce Solutions: How to Make Any Divorce Better

Stoner, Katherine E.
Divorce without Court: A Guide to Mediation & Collaborative Divorce

Trafford, Abigail
Crazy Time: Surviving Divorce and Building a New Life

Ventura, John & Reed, Mary
Divorce for Dummies

Wallerstein, Judith S. & Kelly, John B.
Surviving the Breakup: The Book that Revolutionized America's Thinking about Children and Divorce

Woodhouse, Violet & Collins, Victoria F.
Divorce & Money: How to Make the Best Financial Decisions during Divorce

Whole Person Associates is the leading publisher of training resources for professionals who empower people to create and maintain healthy lifestyles. Our creative resources will help you work effectively with your clients in the areas of stress management, wellness promotion, mental health and life skills.

Please visit us at our web site: **www.wholeperson.com**. You can check out our entire line of products, place an order, request our print catalog, and sign up for our monthly special notifications.

Whole Person Associates

800-247-6789